BEST–LOVED
SLOW COOKER
RECIPES

Publications International, Ltd.

Favorite Brand Name Recipes at www.fbnr.com

Front cover photography by Sanders Studios, Inc.

Pictured on the front cover: Beef Bourguignon *(page 83).*

Pictured on the back cover *(clockwise from top left):*
"Hot" Cheese & Bacon Dip *(page 14),* Peach Crisp *(page 356)* and Chicken in Wine *(page 131).*

ISBN: 0-7853-4102-1

Library of Congress Catalog Card Number: 99-75914

Manufactured in China.

8 7 6 5 4 3 2 1

Microwave Cooking: Microwave ovens vary in wattage. Use the cooking times as guidelines and check for doneness before adding more time.

BEST–LOVED
SLOW COOKER
RECIPES

Slow Cooker

BASICS

Slow cookers can prepare just about any type of food you can imagine. Hearty soups and stews, creative chicken, pork and beef recipes, exciting party ideas and old-fashioned breads and desserts are all included in this publication. Inviting the family over for a relaxed Sunday afternoon meal? Surprise them with Coq au Vin. Have a case of the winter blues? A comforting beef stew is just the thing. Need an easy dessert? Fruit & Nut Baked Apples fit the bill. By following these easy and enticing recipes, you can prepare wonderful meals without a lot of fuss, bother or time.

Slow cookers were introduced in the 1970's and are finding renewed popularity in the 1990's. Considering the hectic pace of today's lifestyle, it's no wonder so many people have rediscovered this time-saving kitchen helper. Spend a few minutes preparing the ingredients, turn on the slow cooker and relax. Low heat and long cooking times take the stress out of meal preparation. Leave for work or a day of leisure and come home 4, 8 or even 10 hours later to a hot, delicious meal.

ABOUT SLOW COOKERS

The original and best-selling slow cooker is the The Rival Company's Crock-Pot® Slow Cooker. The name "Crock-Pot®" is often used interchangeably with "slow cooker." There are two types of slow cookers. The most popular models, including the Crock-Pot® Slow Cooker, have heat coils circling the crockery insert, allowing heat to surround the food and cook evenly. The LOW (about 200°F) and HIGH (about 300°F) settings regulate cooking temperatures. One hour on HIGH equals 2 to 2½ hours on LOW. Less common models of slow cookers have heat coils only on the bottom and have an adjustable thermostat. If you own this type, consult your manufacturer's instructions for advice on converting the recipes in this cookbook.

THE BENEFITS

• No need for constant attention or frequent stirring

• No worry about burning or overcooking

• No sink full of pots and pans to scrub at the end of a long day

• Great for parties and buffets

• Keeps your kitchen cool by keeping your oven turned off

• Saves energy—cooking on the low setting uses less energy than most light bulbs

THE BASICS

• As with conventional cooking recipes, slow cooker recipe time ranges are provided to account for variables such as temperature of ingredients before cooking, how full the slow cooker is and even altitude. Once you become familiar with your slow cooker, you'll have a good idea which end of the range to use.

• Manufacturers recommend that slow cookers should be one-half to three-quarters full for best results.

• Keep a lid on it! The slow cooker can take as long as twenty minutes to regain the heat lost when the cover is removed. If the recipe calls for stirring or checking the dish near the end of the cooking time, replace the lid as quickly as you can.

• To clean your slow cooker, follow the manufacturer's instructions. To make cleanup even easier, spray with nonstick cooking spray before adding food.

• Always taste the finished dish before serving to adjust seasonings to your preference. Consider adding a dash of the following: salt, pepper, seasoned salt, seasoned herb blends, lemon juice, soy sauce, Worcestershire sauce, flavored vinegar, freshly ground pepper or minced fresh herbs.

TIPS AND TECHNIQUES

Adapting Recipes: If you'd like to adapt your own favorite recipe to a slow cooker, you'll need to follow a few guidelines. First, try to find a similar slow cooker recipe in this publication or your manufacturer's guide. Note the cooking times, liquid, quantity and size of meat and vegetable pieces. Because the slow cooker captures moisture, you will want to reduce the amount of liquid, often by as much as half. Add dairy products toward the end of the cooking time so they do not curdle.

BASICS

Follow this chart to estimate the cooking time you will need:

TIME GUIDE

If Recipe Says:	Cook on Low:*	or Cook on High:
15 to 30 minutes	4 to 6 hours	1½ to 2 hours
35 to 45 minutes	6 to 10 hours	3 to 4 hours
50 minutes to 3 hours	8 to 18 hours	4 to 6 hours

Most uncooked meat and vegetable combinations will require at least 8 hours on LOW.

Reprinted with permission from Rival's Crock-Pot® Slow cooker instruction book.

Selecting the Right Meat: A good tip to keep in mind while shopping is that you can, and in fact should, use tougher, inexpensive cuts of meat. Top-quality cuts, such as loin chops or filet mignon, fall apart during long cooking periods and therefore are not great choices to use in the slow cooker. Keep those for roasting, broiling or grilling and save money when you use your slow cooker. You will be amazed to find even the toughest cuts come out fork-tender and flavorful.

Reducing Fat: The slow cooker can help you make lower-fat meals because you won't be cooking in fat as you do when you stir-fry and sauté. And tougher, inexpensive cuts of meat have less fat than prime cuts. Many recipes call for trimming excess fat from meat.

If you do use fatty cuts of meat, such as ribs, consider browning them first on top of the range to cook off excess fat before adding them to the slow cooker.

Chicken skin tends to shrivel and curl in the slow cooker, so most recipes call for skinless chicken. If you use skin-on pieces, brown them before adding them to the slow cooker. If you would rather remove the skin, use the following technique. Freeze the chicken until firm, but not hard. (Do not refreeze thawed chicken.) Grasp the skin with a clean cotton kitchen towel or paper towel and pull away from meat; discard skin. When finished skinning chicken, launder towel before using it again.

You can easily remove most of the fat from accumulated juices, soups and canned broths. The simplest way is to refrigerate the liquid for several hours or overnight. The fat will congeal and float to the top for easy removal. If you plan to use the liquid right away, ladle it into a bowl or measuring cup. Let it stand about 5 minutes so the fat can rise to the surface. Skim with a large spoon. You can also lightly pull a sheet of clean paper towel over the surface, letting the grease be absorbed. To degrease canned broth, refrigerate the unopened can. Simply spoon the congealed fat off the surface after opening the can.

Cutting Your Vegetables: Vegetables often take longer to cook than meats. Cut vegetables into small, thin pieces and place them near the bottom or sides of the slow cooker. Pay careful attention to the recipe instructions in order to cut vegetables to the proper size so they will cook in the amount of time given.

Food Safety Tips: If you do any advance preparation, such as trimming meat or cutting vegetables, make sure you then cover and refrigerate the food until you are ready to start cooking. Store uncooked meats and vegetables separately. If you are preparing meat, poultry or fish, remember to wash your cutting board, utensils and hands with soap and hot water before touching other foods.

Once your dish is cooked, don't keep it in the slow cooker too long. Foods need to be kept cooler than 40°F or hotter than 140°F to avoid the growth of harmful bacteria. Remove food to a clean container, cover and refrigerate as soon as possible. Do not reheat leftovers in the slow cooker. Use a microwave oven, the range-top or the oven for reheating.

Foil to the Rescue: To easily lift a dish or a meatloaf out of the slow cooker, make foil handles according to the following directions.

Photo 1

Photo 2

Photo 1: *Tear off three 18×3-inch strips of heavy-duty foil. Crisscross strips so they resemble spokes of a wheel. Place your dish or food in center of strips.*

Photo 2: *Pull foil strips up and over and place into slow cooker. Leave them in while you cook so you can easily lift item out again when ready.*

By following these simple techniques and using the exciting recipes in this cookbook, you will soon be preparing wonderful dishes with minimal effort.

Slow Cooker

SUPER STARTERS

EASIEST THREE–CHEESE FONDUE

2 cups (8 ounces) shredded mild or sharp Cheddar cheese
¾ cup reduced-fat (2%) milk
1 package (3 ounces) cream cheese, cut into cubes
½ cup (2 ounces) crumbled blue cheese
¼ cup finely chopped onion
1 tablespoon all-purpose flour
1 tablespoon margarine
2 cloves garlic, minced
⅛ teaspoon ground red pepper
4 to 6 drops hot pepper sauce
Bread sticks and assorted fresh vegetables for dipping

Combine all ingredients except dippers in slow cooker. Cover and cook on Low 2 to 2½ hours, stirring once or twice, until cheese is melted and smooth. Increase heat to High and cook 1 to 1½ hours or until heated through. Serve with bread sticks and fresh vegetables. *Makes 8 (3-tablespoon) servings*

HINT: For a special touch, sprinkle fondue with parsley and ground red pepper.

VARIATION: To reduce the total fat, replace the Cheddar cheese and cream cheese with reduced-fat Cheddar and cream cheeses.

CAPONATA

1 medium eggplant (about
     1 pound), peeled and cut
     into 1/2-inch pieces
1 can (14 1/2 ounces) diced Italian
     plum tomatoes, undrained
1 medium onion, chopped
1 red bell pepper, cut into 1/2-inch
     pieces
1/2 cup prepared medium-hot salsa
1/4 cup extra-virgin olive oil
2 tablespoons capers, drained
2 tablespoons balsamic vinegar
3 cloves garlic, minced
1 teaspoon dried oregano leaves
1/4 teaspoon salt
1/3 cup packed fresh basil, cut into
     thin strips
     Toasted sliced Italian or French
     bread

Mix all ingredients except basil and bread in slow cooker. Cover and cook on Low 7 to 8 hours or until vegetables are crisp-tender. Stir in basil. Serve at room temperature on toasted bread.

Makes about 5 1/4 cups

Caponata

HAMBURGER DIP

2 pounds lean ground beef
1 cup chopped onion
2 (8-ounce) cans tomato sauce
2 (8-ounce) packages cream
    cheese, softened, cut into
    cubes
²/₃ cup grated Parmesan cheese
½ cup ketchup
2 cloves garlic, minced *or*
    ¼ teaspoon garlic powder
2 teaspoons sugar
1½ teaspoons dried oregano leaves
1 teaspoon mild chili powder
    Salt to taste

In large skillet, brown ground beef with onion; drain fat. Pour browned meat and onion into CROCK-POT® Slow Cooker. Add tomato sauce, cream cheese, Parmesan cheese, ketchup, garlic, sugar, oregano, chili powder and salt. Set CROCK-POT® Slow Cooker on Low 1½ to 2 hours or until cream cheese has melted and is thoroughly blended. Stir, taste and adjust seasoning, if desired. Serve with cubed French bread or tortilla chips.

Makes about 2 quarts

NOTE: If spicier dip is desired, use hot chili powder in place of mild chili powder.

CHILI CON QUESO

1 pound pasteurized process
    cheese spread, cut into cubes
1 can (10 ounces) diced tomatoes
    and green chiles, undrained
1 cup sliced green onions
2 teaspoons ground coriander
2 teaspoons ground cumin
¾ teaspoon hot pepper sauce

Combine all ingredients in slow cooker until well blended. Cover and cook on Low 2 to 3 hours or until hot.* Garnish with green onion strips and hot pepper slices, if desired.

Makes 3 cups

Chili will be very hot; use caution when serving.

TIP: Serve Chili con Queso with tortilla chips. Or, for something different, cut pita bread into triangles and toast in preheated 400°F oven for 5 minutes or until crisp.

HOT REFRIED BEAN DIP

1 can (16 ounces) refried beans, drained and mashed
¼ pound lean ground beef
3 tablespoons bacon fat
1 pound processed American cheese, cut into cubes
1 to 3 tablespoons taco sauce
1 tablespoon taco seasoning
  Garlic salt to taste

In large skillet, brown beans and ground beef in bacon fat. Add to CROCK-POT® Slow Cooker. Stir in remaining ingredients. Cover and cook on High 1 to 2 hours or until cheese is melted, stirring occasionally. Turn to Low until ready to serve, up to 6 hours. Serve with warm tortilla chips. *Makes about 1½ quarts*

MARINERS' FONDUE

2 cans (10¾ ounces each) condensed cream of celery soup
2 cups (8 ounces) grated sharp processed cheese
1 cup chunked cooked lobster
½ cup chopped cooked shrimp
½ cup chopped cooked crabmeat
¼ cup chopped cooked scallops
  Dash paprika
  Dash cayenne pepper
1 loaf French bread, cut into 1-inch cubes

Combine all ingredients except bread cubes in lightly greased CROCK-POT® Slow Cooker; stir thoroughly. Cover and cook on High 1 hour or until cheese is melted. Turn to Low for serving. Using fondue forks, dip bread cubes into fondue.
Makes about 1½ quarts

13

"HOT" CHEESE AND BACON DIP

16 slices bacon, diced
2 packages (8 ounces each) cream cheese, softened, cut into cubes
4 cups (16 ounces) mild shredded Cheddar cheese
1 cup half-and-half
2 teaspoons Worcestershire sauce
1 teaspoon dried minced onion
½ teaspoon dried mustard
½ teaspoon salt
2 to 3 drops hot pepper sauce

Fry bacon in skillet until crisp; drain on paper towels and set aside. Place cream cheese, Cheddar cheese, half-and-half, Worcestershire sauce, minced onion, mustard, salt and hot pepper sauce in CROCK-POT® Slow Cooker. Set on Low and allow cheese to melt, stirring occasionally, about 1 hour. Taste and adjust seasonings. Stir in bacon and serve directly from CROCK-POT® Slow Cooker. Serve with apple or pear slices or with French bread slices. *Makes 1 quart*

TIP: If serving with fruit slices, dip slices in lemon juice to prevent browning.

"Hot" Cheese and Bacon Dip

HOT BROCCOLI–CHEESE DIP

¾ cup butter
3 stalks celery, thinly sliced
1 medium onion, chopped
1 can (4 ounces) sliced
    mushrooms, drained
3 tablespoons all-purpose flour
1 can (10½ ounces) condensed
    cream of celery soup
1 package (10 ounces) frozen
    broccoli spears or chopped
    broccoli, thawed
1 garlic cheese roll (5 to 6 ounces),
    cut up

In small skillet, melt butter and sauté celery, onion and mushrooms. Stir in flour. Turn into lightly greased CROCK-POT® Slow Cooker; stir in remaining ingredients. Cover and cook on High, stirring about every 15 minutes, until cheese is melted. Turn to Low about 2 to 4 hours or until ready to serve. Serve hot with corn chips, raw cauliflowerets, carrot strips, celery chunks and radishes.

Makes about 1 quart

BBQ MEATBALLS

MEATBALLS

- 2 pounds ground beef
- 1 cup onion-flavored bread crumbs or plain-flavored crumbs
- 2 packages onion soup mix
- 2 eggs
- 2 teaspoons Worcestershire sauce
- 1 teaspoon garlic powder
- 1 tablespoon vegetable oil

In large bowl, combine all ingredients except oil. Shape into meatballs. Brown in skillet with oil. Drain on paper towel.

Makes about 60 meatballs

BBQ SAUCE

- 2 cans (6 ounces each) tomato paste
- 2 large onions, chopped
- $\frac{1}{2}$ cup packed brown sugar
- $\frac{1}{2}$ cup sweet pickle relish
- $\frac{1}{2}$ cup beef broth
- $\frac{1}{4}$ cup red wine vinegar
- $\frac{1}{4}$ cup Worcestershire sauce
- 2 teaspoons salt
- 2 teaspoons dried mustard
- 2 cloves garlic, minced

Add sauce ingredients to CROCK-POT® Slow Cooker and stir well. Place meatballs in CROCK-POT® Slow Cooker and cook on Low 5 to 6 hours or on High 2 to 3 hours or until hot. Serve directly from CROCK-POT® Slow Cooker.

BARBECUED MEATBALLS

2 pounds lean ground beef
1⅓ cups ketchup, divided
3 tablespoons seasoned dry bread
    crumbs
1 egg, lightly beaten
2 tablespoons dried onion flakes
¾ teaspoon garlic salt
½ teaspoon black pepper
1 cup packed brown sugar
1 can (6 ounces) tomato paste
¼ cup reduced-sodium soy sauce
¼ cup cider vinegar
1½ teaspoons hot pepper sauce
    Diced bell peppers (optional)

Preheat oven to 350°F. Combine ground beef, ⅓ cup ketchup, bread crumbs, egg, onion flakes, garlic salt and black pepper in medium bowl. Mix lightly but thoroughly; shape into 1-inch meatballs. Place meatballs in two 15×10-inch jelly-roll pans or shallow roasting pans. Bake 18 minutes or until browned. Transfer meatballs to slow cooker.

Mix remaining 1 cup ketchup, sugar, tomato paste, soy sauce, vinegar and hot pepper sauce in medium bowl. Pour over meatballs. Cover and cook on Low 4 hours. Serve with cocktail picks. Garnish with bell peppers, if desired.

Makes about 4 dozen meatballs

BARBECUED FRANKS: Arrange 2 (12-ounce) packages *or* 3 (8-ounce) packages cocktail franks in slow cooker. Combine 1 cup ketchup with sugar, tomato paste, soy sauce, vinegar and hot pepper sauce; pour over franks. Cook according to directions for Barbecued Meatballs.

Barbecued Meatballs

TURKEY MEATBALLS IN CRANBERRY–BARBECUE SAUCE

1 can (16 ounces) jellied
    cranberry sauce
½ cup barbecue sauce
1 egg white
1 pound ground turkey
1 green onion with top, sliced
2 teaspoons grated orange peel
1 teaspoon reduced-sodium soy
    sauce
¼ teaspoon black pepper
⅛ teaspoon ground red pepper
    (optional)

Combine cranberry sauce and barbecue sauce in slow cooker. Cover and cook on High 20 to 30 minutes or until cranberry sauce is melted and mixture is hot, stirring every 10 minutes.

Meanwhile, place egg white in medium bowl; beat lightly. Add turkey, green onion, orange peel, soy sauce, black pepper and ground red pepper, if desired; mix well with hands until well blended. Shape into 24 balls.

Spray large nonstick skillet with nonstick cooking spray. Add meatballs to skillet; cook over medium heat 8 to 10 minutes or until meatballs are no longer pink in center, carefully turning occasionally to brown evenly. Add to heated sauce in slow cooker; stir gently to coat evenly with sauce.

Reduce heat to Low. Cover and cook 3 hours. When ready to serve, transfer meatballs to serving plate; garnish, if desired. Serve with decorative picks. *Makes 12 servings*

Turkey Meatballs in Cranberry–Barbecue Sauce

SPICY FRANKS

1 cup ketchup
¼ cup firmly packed light brown
    sugar
1 tablespoon red wine vinegar
2 teaspoons soy sauce
2 teaspoons Dijon mustard
⅛ teaspoon garlic powder
1 pound frankfurters, cut into
    1-inch pieces *or* 1 pound
    cocktail wieners or smoked
    sausages

Place ketchup, brown sugar, vinegar, soy sauce, mustard and garlic powder in CROCK-POT® Slow Cooker. Cover and cook on High until blended, 1 to 2 hours. Stir in frankfurters. Cook 1 to 2 hours until thoroughly heated. Turn to Low to keep warm and serve from CROCK-POT® Slow Cooker.   *Makes 6 to 8 servings*

CHICKEN WINGS IN TERIYAKI SAUCE

3 pounds chicken wings
    (16 wings)
1 large onion, chopped
1 cup brown sugar
1 cup soy sauce
¼ cup dry cooking sherry
2 teaspoons ground ginger
2 cloves garlic, minced

Rinse chicken and pat dry. Cut off and discard wing tips. Cut each wing at joint to make two sections. Place wing parts on broiler pan. Broil 4 to 5 inches from heat 20 minutes, 10 minutes a side or until chicken is brown. Transfer chicken to CROCK-POT® Slow Cooker.

Mix together onion, brown sugar, soy sauce, cooking sherry, ginger and garlic in bowl. Pour over chicken wings. Cover and cook on Low 5 to 6 hours or on High 2 to 3 hours. Stir chicken wings once to ensure wings are evenly coated with sauce. Serve from CROCK-POT® Slow Cooker.   *Makes about 32 appetizers*

Chicken Wings in Teriyaki Sauce

CHICKEN WINGS IN HONEY SAUCE

**3 pounds chicken wings
    (16 wings)**
Salt and black pepper to taste
2 cups honey
1 cup soy sauce
½ cup ketchup
¼ cup oil
2 cloves garlic, minced
Sesame seeds (optional)

Rinse chicken and pat dry. Cut off and discard wing tips. Cut each wing at joint to make two sections. Sprinkle wing parts with salt and pepper. Place wings on broiler pan. Broil 4 to 5 inches from heat 20 minutes, 10 minutes a side or until chicken is brown. Transfer chicken to CROCK-POT® Slow Cooker.

For sauce, combine honey, soy sauce, ketchup, oil and garlic in bowl. Pour over chicken wings. Cover and cook on Low 4 to 5 hours or on High 2 to 2½ hours. Garnish with sesame seeds, if desired. *Makes about 32 appetizers*

CHICKEN WINGS IN BBQ SAUCE

**3 pounds chicken wings
    (16 wings)**
Salt and black pepper to taste
1½ cups any variety barbecue sauce
¼ cup honey
**2 teaspoons prepared mustard or
    spicy mustard**
2 teaspoons Worcestershire sauce
Hot pepper sauce to taste
    (optional)

Rinse chicken and pat dry. Cut off and discard wing tips. Cut each wing at joint to make two sections. Sprinkle wing parts with salt and pepper. Place wings on broiler pan. Broil 4 to 5 inches from heat 20 minutes, 10 minutes a side or until chicken is brown. Transfer chicken to CROCK-POT® Slow Cooker.

For sauce, combine barbecue sauce, honey, mustard, Worcestershire sauce and hot pepper sauce, if desired, in small bowl. Pour over chicken wings. Cover and cook on Low 4 to 5 hours or on High 2 to 2½ hours. Serve directly from CROCK-POT® Slow Cooker.
Makes about 32 appetizers

Chicken Wings in Honey Sauce

PARTY MIX

3 cups bite-size rice cereal
2 cups O-shaped oat cereal
2 cups bite-size shredded wheat
   cereal
1 cup peanuts, pecans or cashews
1 cup thin pretzel sticks
   (optional)
½ cup butter or margarine, melted
4 tablespoons Worcestershire
   sauce
½ teaspoon seasoned salt
½ teaspoon garlic salt
½ teaspoon onion salt
   Dash hot pepper sauce

Combine cereals, nuts and pretzels in CROCK-POT® Slow Cooker. Mix melted butter with remaining ingredients in small bowl; pour over cereal mixture in CROCK-POT® Slow Cooker and toss lightly to coat. *Do not cover CROCK-POT® Slow Cooker.* Cook on High 2 hours, stirring well every 30 minutes; turn to Low for 2 to 6 hours. Store in airtight container. *Makes 10 cups*

Party Mix

MULLED APPLE CIDER

2 quarts bottled apple cider or
   juice (not unfiltered)
¼ cup packed brown sugar
1 square (8 inches) double-
   thickness cheesecloth
8 allspice berries
4 cinnamon sticks, broken into
   halves
12 whole cloves
1 large orange
   Additional cinnamon sticks
   (optional)

Combine apple cider and brown sugar in slow cooker. Rinse cheesecloth; squeeze out water. Wrap allspice berries and cinnamon stick halves in cheesecloth; tie securely with cotton string or strip of cheesecloth. Stick cloves randomly into orange; cut orange into quarters. Place spice bag and orange quarters in cider mixture. Cover and cook on High 2½ to 3 hours. Once cooked, cider may be turned to Low and kept warm up to 3 additional hours. Discard spice bag and orange before serving; ladle cider into mugs. Garnish with additional cinnamon sticks, if desired.
Makes 10 servings

TIP: To make inserting cloves into the orange a little easier, first pierce the orange skin with the point of wooden skewer. Remove the skewer and insert a clove.

Mulled Apple Cider

SUPER STARTERS

HOT CRANBERRY PUNCH

4 cups unsweetened pineapple
    juice
4 cups cranberry juice
½ cup packed brown sugar
1 cup water
1 teaspoon whole cloves *and*
    1 cinnamon stick tied in
    cheesecloth
1 to 2 cups vodka

Combine all ingredients except vodka in CROCK-POT® Slow Cooker. Cover and cook on Low 4 to 10 hours. Add vodka before serving. Serve hot, in punch cups.

Makes 10 to 15 servings (about 2½ quarts)

HOT SPICED CHERRY CIDER

3½ quarts apple cider
2 cinnamon sticks
2 packages (3 ounces each)
    cherry-flavored gelatin

In 4-, 5- or 6-quart CROCK-POT® Slow Cooker, mix together apple cider and cinnamon sticks. Heat on High 3 hours. Stir in cherry-flavored gelatin. Keep on High 1 more hour and allow gelatin to dissolve. Turn to Low to keep warm. Serve directly from CROCK-POT® Slow Cooker. *Makes about 3½ quarts*

SUPER STARTERS

SPICED APPLE TEA

3 bags cinnamon herbal tea
3 cups boiling water
2 cups unsweetened apple juice
6 whole cloves
1 cinnamon stick

Place tea bags in slow cooker. Pour boiling water over tea bags; cover and let stand 10 minutes. Remove and discard tea bags. Add apple juice, cloves and cinnamon stick to slow cooker. Cover and cook on Low 2 to 3 hours. Remove and discard cloves and cinnamon stick. Serve in warm mugs.   *Makes 4 servings*

ORANGE–CIDER PUNCH

6 cups orange juice
2 cups apple cider or apple juice
1 cup sugar
2 cinnamon sticks
1 whole nutmeg
2 cups vodka (optional)

Mix all ingredients except vodka in CROCK-POT® Slow Cooker; stir well. Cover and cook on Low 4 to 10 hours or on High 2 to 3 hours. Just before serving, stir in vodka. Serve hot, in punch cups.   *Makes 10 to 15 servings (about 2½ quarts)*

VIENNESE COFFEE

3 cups strong freshly brewed hot
    coffee
3 tablespoons chocolate syrup
1 teaspoon sugar
⅓ cup heavy cream
¼ cup crème de cacao or Irish
    cream (optional)
    Whipped cream
    Chocolate shavings for garnish

Combine coffee, chocolate syrup and sugar in slow cooker. Cover and cook on Low 2 to 2½ hours. Stir in heavy cream and crème de cacao, if desired. Cover and cook 30 minutes or until heated through.

Ladle coffee into coffee cups, top with whipped cream and chocolate shavings. *Makes about 4 servings*

Viennese Coffee

MOCHA SUPREME

2 quarts brewed strong coffee
**½ cup instant hot chocolate
  beverage mix**
**1 cinnamon stick, broken into
  halves**
1 cup whipping cream
1 tablespoon powdered sugar

Place coffee, hot chocolate mix and cinnamon stick halves in slow cooker; stir. Cover and cook on High 2 to 2½ hours or until hot. Remove and discard cinnamon stick halves.

Beat cream in medium bowl with electric mixer on high speed until soft peaks form. Add powdered sugar; beat until stiff peaks form. Ladle hot beverage into mugs; top with whipped cream.

Makes 8 servings

HINT: You can whip cream faster if you first chill the beaters and bowls in the freezer for 15 minutes.

HOT MULLED CIDER

½ gallon apple cider
½ cup packed light brown sugar
**½ cup applejack or bourbon
  (optional)**
**1½ teaspoons balsamic or cider
  vinegar**
1 teaspoon vanilla
1 cinnamon stick
6 whole cloves

Combine all ingredients in slow cooker. Cover and cook on Low 5 to 6 hours. Discard cinnamon stick and cloves. Serve in mugs.

Makes 16 servings

Mocha Supreme

MULLED WINE

2 bottles (750 ml each) dry red
    wine, such as Cabernet
    Sauvignon
1 cup light corn syrup
1 cup water
1 square (8 inches) double-
    thickness cheesecloth
  Peel of 1 large orange
1 cinnamon stick, broken into
    halves
8 whole cloves
1 whole nutmeg

Combine wine, corn syrup and water in slow cooker. Rinse cheesecloth; squeeze out water. Wrap orange peel, cinnamon stick halves, cloves and nutmeg in cheesecloth. Tie securely with cotton string or strip of cheesecloth. Add to slow cooker. Cover and cook on High 2 to 2½ hours. Discard spice bag; ladle into mugs. *Makes 12 servings*

SPICY PEACH PUNCH

1 bottle (46 ounces) peach nectar
1 bottle (20 ounces) orange juice
½ cup plus 2 tablespoons light
    brown sugar
1 cinnamon stick
¾ teaspoon whole cloves
1 tablespoon lime juice

Combine peach nectar, orange juice and 2 tablespoons sugar in CROCK-POT® Slow Cooker. Tie spices in cheesecloth bag or add loosely to punch. Cover and set on Low 2 hours or on High 1 hour. Stir in remaining ½ cup sugar and lime juice. Allow sugar to dissolve, approximately 30 minutes. Adjust spices to taste. Turn to Low to keep punch warm. Serve directly from CROCK-POT® Slow Cooker. *Makes about 2 quarts*

Mulled Wine

HOT CRANBERRY TEA

1 package (8 ounces) fresh
  cranberries
3 quarts water, divided
2 cups sugar
1 cup cinnamon red hots
24 whole cloves
3 cinnamon sticks
  Juice from 3 oranges
  Juice from 3 lemons

Boil cranberries in 1 quart water 10 minutes; set aside. Mix remaining 2 quarts water, sugar, red hots, cloves and cinnamon sticks in 4-, 5- or 6-quart CROCK-POT® Slow Cooker. Cover and heat on High approximately 1 hour or until red hots dissolve. Strain cranberry mixture and stir into CROCK-POT® Slow Cooker. Stir in juice from oranges and lemons. Cover and heat on High 2 hours; turn to Low to keep warm and serve directly from CROCK-POT® Slow Cooker. *Makes about 4 quarts*

HOT SPICED WINE

2 bottles (750 ml each) dry red
  wine
3 apples, peeled, cored and thinly
  sliced
½ cup sugar
1 teaspoon lemon juice
2 cinnamon sticks
3 whole cloves

Combine all ingredients in CROCK-POT® Slow Cooker; stir well. Cover and cook on Low 4 to 12 hours or on High 1 to 2 hours. Serve hot, in punch cups or mugs.
Makes 8 to 12 servings (about 2 quarts)

WARM FRUIT PUNCH

8 cups water
1 can (12 ounces) frozen
    cranberry-raspberry juice
    concentrate, thawed
1 can (12 ounces) frozen orange
    juice concentrate, thawed
1 can (6 ounces) frozen lemonade
    concentrate, thawed
$\frac{1}{2}$ cup sugar
4 cinnamon sticks
$\frac{1}{4}$ teaspoon whole cloves
$\frac{1}{4}$ teaspoon whole allspice
    Thin orange slice halves,
      unpeeled, for garnish

In 6-quart CROCK-POT® Slow Cooker, combine all ingredients except orange slices. (The spices can be tied in a cheesecloth bag and placed in punch, if desired.) Cover and heat on High 3 hours; turn to Low. Remove spices from CROCK-POT® Slow Cooker with small strainer or slotted spoon. Serve directly from CROCK-POT® Slow Cooker. Garnish with orange slice halves, if desired.

Makes about 2½ quarts

Slow Cooker

SAVORY SOUPS

COUNTRY CHICKEN CHOWDER

  2 tablespoons margarine or butter
1½ pounds chicken tenders, cut into ½-inch pieces
  2 cans (10¾ ounces each) cream of potato soup
  2 cups frozen corn
1½ cups chicken broth
  2 small onions, chopped
  2 ribs celery, sliced
  2 small carrots, sliced
  1 teaspoon dried dill weed
  ½ cup half-and-half

Melt margarine in large skillet. Add chicken; cook until browned. Add cooked chicken, soup, corn, chicken broth, onions, celery, carrots and dill to slow cooker. Cover and cook on Low 3 to 4 hours or until chicken is no longer pink and vegetables are tender.

Turn off heat; stir in half-and-half. Cover and let stand 5 to 10 minutes or just until heated through. *Makes 8 servings*

NOTE: For a special touch, garnish soup with croutons and fresh dill.

CHICKEN AND VEGETABLE CHOWDER

1 pound boneless skinless chicken breasts, cut into 1-inch pieces
10 ounces frozen broccoli cuts
1 can (14½ ounces) reduced-sodium chicken broth
1 can (10¾ ounces) condensed cream of potato soup
1 cup sliced carrots
1 jar (4½ ounces) sliced mushrooms, drained
½ cup chopped onion
½ cup whole kernel corn
2 cloves garlic, minced
½ teaspoon dried thyme leaves
⅓ cup half-and-half

Combine all ingredients except half-and-half in slow cooker. Cover and cook on Low 5 hours or until vegetables are tender and chicken is no longer pink in center. Stir in half-and-half. Turn to High. Cover and cook 15 minutes or until heated through.

Makes 6 servings

VARIATION: If desired, ½ cup (2 ounces) shredded Swiss or Cheddar cheese can be added. Add to thickened broth and half-and-half, stirring over Low heat until melted.

Chicken and Vegetable Chowder

CHICKEN TORTILLA SOUP

1½ pounds boneless chicken,
    cooked and shredded
1 can (15 ounces) whole tomatoes
1 can (10 ounces) enchilada sauce
1 medium onion, chopped
1 can (4 ounces) chopped green
    chilies
1 clove garlic, minced
2 cups water
1 can (14½ ounces) chicken broth
1 teaspoon ground cumin
1 teaspoon chili powder
1 teaspoon salt
¼ teaspoon black pepper
1 bay leaf
1 package (10 ounces) frozen corn
1 tablespoon dried chopped
    cilantro
6 corn tortillas
2 tablespoons vegetable oil
    Grated Parmesan cheese for
    garnish

In CROCK-POT® Slow Cooker, combine shredded chicken, whole tomatoes, enchilada sauce, onion, green chilies and garlic. Add water, chicken broth, cumin, chili powder, salt, black pepper and bay leaf. Stir in corn and cilantro. Cover and cook on Low 6 to 8 hours or on High 3 to 4 hours. Remove and discard bay leaf.

Preheat oven to 400°F. Lightly brush both sides of tortillas with vegetable oil. Cut tortillas into 2½×½-inch strips. Spread tortilla strips onto baking sheet. Bake, turning occasionally, until crisp, 5 to 10 minutes. Sprinkle tortilla strips and grated Parmesan cheese over soup. Serve immediately. *Makes 6 to 8 servings*

CHICKEN AND SAUSAGE GUMBO

½ pound smoked sausage, sliced
1 cup chopped onion
½ cup chopped green bell pepper
¾ pound chicken breasts, cooked
   and shredded
8 cups water
¾ cup all-purpose flour
½ cup chopped celery
1 tablespoon Worcestershire
   sauce
2 cloves garlic, minced
1½ teaspoons Cajun seasoning
1 teaspoon salt
½ teaspoon dried thyme leaves
¼ teaspoon black pepper
1 bay leaf
   Dash hot sauce
4 cups hot cooked rice
¾ cup sliced green onions

Brown sausage, onion and bell pepper in skillet. Drain fat. In CROCK-POT® Slow Cooker, combine sausage mixture, shredded chicken, water, flour, celery and seasonings. Cover and cook on Low 6 to 8 hours or on High 3 to 4 hours. Serve over rice and garnish with green onions. *Makes 8 to 10 servings*

SAVORY SOUPS

CHICKEN AND RICE SOUP

1 pound boneless skinless
  chicken breasts, cooked and
  cut into pieces
3 cans (14½ ounces each) chicken
  broth
2 cups frozen mixed vegetables
¾ cup uncooked converted white
  rice
½ cup sliced celery
½ cup water
1 tablespoon parsley flakes
2 teaspoons lemon and herb
  seasoning

Combine all ingredients in CROCK-POT® Slow Cooker. Cover and cook on Low 6 to 8 hours or on High 3 to 4 hours. Serve.

Makes 4 to 6 servings

NOTE: If cooking on High, place celery in dish in microwave with 1 tablespoon water and cover. Microwave until celery is slightly soft, then add to CROCK-POT® Slow Cooker and cook on High.

HINT: If soup is a little too thick, add more water for a thinner soup. Allow to cook 15 minutes.

BEEF STOCK

3 beef soup bones
1 to 2 onions, chopped
1 to 2 carrots, peeled and
  chopped
2 stalks celery, chopped
2 tablespoons dried parsley flakes
2 teaspoons salt
2 peppercorns

Place all ingredients in CROCK-POT® Slow Cooker. Add enough water to cover all ingredients. Cover and cook on Low 12 to 24 hours or on High 4 to 6 hours. If cooked on High, the stock will be lighter in color and less concentrated. Strain and refrigerate. Keeps well 4 to 5 days or may be frozen.

Makes 8 cups strained stock

VEAL STOCK: Substitute veal bones for the beef bones.

REUBEN SOUP

1 cup chopped onion
1 cup chopped celery
¼ cup margarine or butter
2 cups chicken broth
2 cups beef broth
1 teaspoon baking soda
¼ cup cornstarch
¼ cup water
4 cups milk
4 cups chopped cooked corned
   beef
1½ cups sauerkraut, rinsed and
   drained
2 cups shredded Swiss cheese
   Salt
   Black pepper
   Rye croutons (optional)

Place onion, celery and margarine in CROCK-POT® Slow Cooker. Stir in broths and baking soda. Combine cornstarch and water and add to CROCK-POT® Slow Cooker. Stir in milk, corned beef and sauerkraut. Cover and cook on High 4 to 5 hours. Stir in cheese and cook 30 minutes. Season with salt and pepper. Serve. Garnish with croutons, if desired. *Makes 12 servings*

SAVORY PEA SOUP WITH SAUSAGE

8 ounces smoked sausage, cut lengthwise into halves, then cut into ½-inch pieces
2 cans (14½ ounces each) reduced-sodium chicken broth
1 package (16 ounces) dried split peas, sorted and rinsed
3 medium carrots, sliced
2 ribs celery, sliced
1 medium onion, chopped
¾ teaspoon dried marjoram leaves
1 bay leaf

Heat small skillet over medium heat. Add sausage; cook 5 to 8 minutes or until browned. Drain well. Combine sausage and remaining ingredients in slow cooker. Cover and cook on Low 4 to 5 hours or until peas are tender. Turn off heat. Remove and discard bay leaf. Cover and let stand 15 minutes to thicken.

Makes 6 servings

Savory Pea Soup with Sausage

THREE BEAN TURKEY SOUP

1 pound ground turkey
1 cup chopped onion
¾ cup chopped green bell pepper
2 cloves garlic, minced
1 can (16 ounces) red kidney
    beans, drained
1 can (16 ounces) Great Northern
    beans or pinto beans, drained
1 can (16 ounces) black beans
2 cans (14½ ounces) whole
    tomatoes, undrained and
    chopped
3 cups water
1 can (8 ounces) tomato sauce
2 cups sliced carrots
2 teaspoons dried oregano leaves
½ teaspoon dried thyme leaves
½ teaspoon chicken-flavored
    bouillon granules
½ teaspoon salt
½ teaspoon black pepper

In large skillet, brown turkey, onion, bell pepper and garlic. Drain fat. Transfer to CROCK-POT® Slow Cooker. Add beans, tomatoes, water, tomato sauce, carrots and seasonings. Stir. Cover and cook on Low 8 to 10 hours or on High 4 to 5 hours. Before serving, mash beans slightly for a thicker soup, if desired. Serve. *Makes 10 to 12 servings*

LAMB MEATBALL & BEAN SOUP

1 pound ground lamb
¼ cup chopped onion
1 clove garlic, minced
1 teaspoon ground cumin
½ teaspoon salt
2 cups chicken broth
1 (15-ounce) can diced tomatoes, drained
1 (15-ounce) can garbanzo beans or black-eyed peas, drained
1 (10-ounce) package frozen chopped broccoli*
½ teaspoon dried thyme leaves, crushed
Salt and black pepper

Substitute 1½ cups fresh broccoli flowerets for 10-ounce package frozen chopped broccoli.

Combine lamb, onion, garlic, cumin and salt; mix lightly. Shape into 1-inch balls. Brown meatballs in large skillet over medium-high heat, turning occasionally.

Place broth, tomatoes, beans, broccoli, thyme and meatballs in slow cooker. Cook on Low 4 to 5 hours. Season with salt and pepper to taste. *Makes 4 to 6 servings*

SMOKED SAUSAGE GUMBO

1 can (14½ ounces) diced
   tomatoes, undrained
1 cup chicken broth
¼ cup all-purpose flour
2 tablespoons olive oil
¾ pound Polish sausage, cut into
   ½-inch pieces
1 medium onion, diced
1 green bell pepper, diced
2 ribs celery, chopped
1 carrot, peeled and chopped
2 teaspoons dried oregano leaves
2 teaspoons dried thyme leaves
⅛ teaspoon ground red pepper
1 cup uncooked long-grain white
   rice

Combine tomatoes and broth in slow cooker. Sprinkle flour evenly over bottom of small skillet. Cook over high heat without stirring 3 to 4 minutes or until flour begins to brown. Reduce heat to medium; stir flour about 4 minutes. Stir in oil until smooth. Carefully whisk flour mixture into slow cooker.

Add sausage, onion, bell pepper, celery, carrot, oregano, thyme and ground red pepper to slow cooker. Stir well. Cover and cook on Low 4½ to 5 hours or until juices are thickened.

About 30 minutes before gumbo is ready to serve, prepare rice. Cook rice in 2 cups boiling water in medium saucepan. Serve gumbo over rice. *Makes 4 servings*

HINT: For a special touch, sprinkle chopped parsley over each serving.

NOTE: If gumbo thickens upon standing, stir in additional broth.

Smoked Sausage Gumbo

SPICY CABBAGE–BEEF SOUP

1 pound ground beef
1 large onion, chopped
5 cups chopped cabbage
    (bite-size pieces)
2 cans (16 ounces each) red
    kidney beans
3 cans (8 ounces each) tomato
    sauce
2 cups water
1 green bell pepper, chopped
3/4 cup picante sauce
4 beef bouillon cubes
1 1/2 teaspoons ground cumin
1/2 teaspoon salt
1/4 teaspoon black pepper

Brown ground beef and onion over medium heat in large skillet; drain. Pour into CROCK-POT® Slow Cooker. Stir in cabbage, beans, tomato sauce, water, bell pepper, picante sauce, bouillon cubes and seasonings. Cover and cook on Low 6 to 8 hours or on High 3 to 4 hours. Serve when cabbage is tender.

Makes 10 to 12 servings

MINESTRONE HAMBURGER SOUP

1 pound lean ground beef
1 can (28 ounces) whole tomatoes
1 cup shredded cabbage
1 large onion, chopped
2 small potatoes, peeled and
    cubed
2 carrots, peeled and sliced
2 stalks celery, sliced
1 small bay leaf
1 teaspoon salt
$\frac{1}{4}$ teaspoon dried thyme leaves
$\frac{1}{4}$ teaspoon dried basil leaves
$\frac{1}{4}$ teaspoon black pepper
    Grated mozzarella or Parmesan
        cheese

Place all ingredients except cheese in CROCK-POT® Slow Cooker; stir thoroughly. Add enough water to cover all ingredients. Cover and cook on Low 8 to 12 hours or on High 3 to 5 hours. Stir well. Serve sprinkled with cheese. *Makes 6 servings*

SAUSAGE–BEAN SOUP

1 pound bulk Italian sausage or
  kielbasa cut into pieces
½ cup chopped onion
2 cloves garlic, minced
1 can (16 ounces) whole
  tomatoes, undrained, cut up
1 can (15 ounces) black beans,
  undrained
1 can (15 ounces) butter beans,
  undrained
1 can (14½ ounces) beef broth
1 teaspoon dried basil leaves
  Grated Parmesan cheese for
  garnish

In skillet, brown sausage, onion and garlic. Drain fat. Transfer to CROCK-POT® Slow Cooker. Stir in remaining ingredients except Parmesan cheese. Cover and cook on Low 6 to 8 hours or on High 3 to 4 hours. Ladle into bowls and top each serving with Parmesan cheese, if desired. *Makes 6 servings*

FISHERMAN'S CATCH CHOWDER

1 to 1½ pounds fish (use any combination of the following: flounder, ocean perch, pike, rainbow trout, haddock or halibut)
1 can (16 ounces) whole tomatoes, mashed
1 bottle (8 ounces) clam juice
½ cup chopped onion
½ cup chopped celery
½ cup chopped peeled carrots
½ cup dry white wine
¼ cup snipped parsley
1 teaspoon salt
¼ teaspoon dried rosemary
⅓ cup light cream
3 tablespoons all-purpose flour
3 tablespoons butter or margarine, melted

Cut cleaned fish into 1-inch pieces. Combine all ingredients except cream, flour and butter in CROCK-POT® Slow Cooker; stir well. Cover and cook on Low 7 to 8 hours or on High 3 to 4 hours.

One hour before serving, combine cream, flour and butter. Stir into fish mixture. Continue to cook until mixture is slightly thickened. *Makes 4 servings*

NOTE: Double recipe for 5-quart CROCK-POT® Slow Cooker.

MEDITERRANEAN FISH SOUP

2 cans (14½ ounces each)
    reduced-sodium chicken
    broth
1 can (14½ ounces) whole
    tomatoes, undrained and
    coarsely chopped
1 can (8 ounces) tomato sauce
1 medium onion, chopped
½ medium green bell pepper,
    chopped
½ cup orange juice
½ cup dry white wine (optional)
1 jar (2½ ounces) sliced
    mushrooms
¼ cup black olives, sliced
2 cloves garlic, minced
2 bay leaves
1 teaspoon dried basil leaves
¼ teaspoon fennel seeds, crushed
⅛ teaspoon black pepper
1 pound uncooked medium
    shrimp, peeled and deveined

Place all ingredients except shrimp in slow cooker. Cover and cook on Low 4 to 4½ hours or until vegetables are crisp-tender. Stir in shrimp. Cover and cook 15 to 30 minutes or until shrimp are opaque. Remove and discard bay leaves.   *Makes 6 servings*

NOTE: If you prefer a hearty soup, add more fish. Cut 1 pound of whitefish or cod into 1-inch pieces. Add the fish to slow cooker 45 minutes before serving. Cover and cook on Low.

Mediterranean Fish Soup

CIOPPINO

1 pound sea bass, cut into
    chunks, divided
1 can (4 ounces) sliced
    mushrooms, undrained
2 carrots, peeled and sliced
1 medium onion, chopped
1 small green bell pepper, seeded
    and chopped
1 clove garlic, minced
1 can (15 ounces) tomato sauce
1 can (14 ounces) beef broth
  Salt to taste
½ teaspoon dried oregano leaves
⅛ teaspoon seasoned black pepper
1 can (7 ounces) clams,
    undrained
½ pound shelled deveined shrimp
1 small lobster tail (optional)
1 package (6 ounces) frozen
    crabmeat, thawed and
    cartilage removed
  Minced parsley

Combine half of sea bass in CROCK-POT® Slow Cooker with vegetables, garlic, tomato sauce, beef broth and seasonings; stir well. Cover and cook on Low 10 to 12 hours or on High 2 to 4 hours.

One hour before serving, turn to High and stir in remaining sea bass and seafood. Cover and cook on High 1 hour or until done.

Garnish with minced parsley and serve in soup plates. Accompany with hot Italian bread. *Makes 6 servings*

POTATO AND MUSHROOM CHOWDER

1 cup chopped celery
½ cup chopped onion
¼ cup margarine or butter
2 tablespoons all-purpose flour
1 teaspoon salt
½ teaspoon black pepper
2 cups water
2 cups diced peeled potatoes
2 cans (4 ounces each) sliced
    mushrooms, drained
1 cup chopped carrots
2 cups milk
¼ cup grated Parmesan cheese

In skillet, sauté celery and onion in margarine until onion is translucent. Remove from heat. Add flour, salt and pepper; stir. Place in CROCK-POT® Slow Cooker. Add water; stir in potatoes, mushrooms and carrots. Cover and cook on Low 6 to 8 hours or on High 3 to 4 hours. If on Low turn to High. Add milk and Parmesan cheese and cook 30 minutes. Serve.

Makes 4 servings

HINT: Use 2 cups frozen hash browns and 1 cup frozen carrots (in place of fresh potatoes and carrots) and cook on High 2 to 3 hours.

CREAMY VEGETABLE SOUP

3 medium sweet potatoes, peeled and chopped
3 zucchini, chopped
1 to 2 cups chopped broccoli
1 large onion, chopped
¼ cup margarine or butter, melted
3 cans (14½ ounces each) chicken broth
2 medium baking potatoes, peeled and shredded
2 teaspoons salt
1 teaspoon ground cumin
1 teaspoon black pepper
½ teaspoon celery seeds
2 cups milk

In CROCK-POT® Slow Cooker, stir together sweet potatoes, zucchini, broccoli, onion and margarine. Pour in chicken broth and stir. Add baking potatoes and seasonings. Stir. Cover and cook on Low 8 to 10 hours or on High 4 to 5 hours. Add milk and cook 30 minutes to 1 hour. Serve. *Makes 12 servings*

Creamy Vegetable Soup

GERMAN POTATO SOUP

1 pound potatoes, diced
4 cups beef broth
1 onion, chopped
1 leek, trimmed and diced
2 carrots, peeled and diced
1 cup chopped cabbage
¼ cup chopped parsley
1 bay leaf
2 teaspoons black pepper
1 teaspoon salt
½ teaspoon caraway seeds
¼ teaspoon ground nutmeg
½ cup sour cream
1 pound bacon, cooked and diced

Combine potatoes, broth, onion, leek, carrots, cabbage and parsley in CROCK-POT® Slow Cooker. Stir in seasonings. Cover and cook on Low 8 to 10 hours or on High 4 to 5 hours. Remove and discard bay leaf. Using slotted spoon remove potatoes and mash. Combine potatoes with sour cream. Return to CROCK-POT® Slow Cooker and stir. Stir in bacon pieces. Serve.

Makes 6 to 8 servings

NOTE: For 6-quart CROCK-POT® Slow Cooker, use 6 cups beef broth, 2 leeks, 3 carrots and 2 pounds potatoes. Season as desired.

German Potato Soup

NAVY BEAN BACON CHOWDER

1½ cups dried navy beans, rinsed
2 cups cold water
6 slices thick-cut bacon
1 medium carrot, cut lengthwise into halves, then cut into 1-inch pieces
1 rib celery, chopped
1 medium onion, chopped
1 small turnip, cut into 1-inch pieces
1 teaspoon dried Italian seasoning
⅛ teaspoon black pepper
1 large can (46 ounces) reduced-sodium chicken broth
1 cup milk

Soak beans overnight in cold water.

Cook bacon in medium skillet over medium heat. Drain and crumble. Combine carrot, celery, onion, turnip, Italian seasoning, pepper, beans and bacon in slow cooker; mix slightly. Pour broth over top. Cover and cook on Low 7½ to 9 hours or until beans are crisp-tender.

Ladle 2 cups of soup mixture into food processor or blender. Process until smooth; return to slow cooker. Add milk; cover and heat on High 10 minutes or until heated through.

Makes 6 servings

Navy Bean Bacon Chowder

SAVORY SOUPS

CORN CHOWDER

2½ cups milk
1 can (10¾ ounces) cream of
    mushroom soup, undiluted
1 package (10 ounces) frozen corn
1 cup cream-style corn
1 cup frozen hash brown potatoes
1 cup diced cooked ham
¾ cup chopped onion
2 tablespoons margarine or butter
  Salt
  Black pepper
  Chopped parsley

Combine milk, soup, corn, potatoes, ham, onion and margarine in CROCK-POT® Slow Cooker. Cover and cook on High 4 to 5 hours. Add salt and pepper to taste. Garnish with parsley. Serve.

Makes 8 servings

OLD–FASHIONED ONION SOUP

3 pounds large onions, peeled
    and thinly sliced
½ cup butter, melted
6 to 8 slices French bread, cubed
4 to 5 cups chicken broth

Place sliced onions in CROCK-POT® Slow Cooker; pour in butter and mix to coat onions thoroughly. Stir in cubed bread. Add chicken broth to cover; stir well. Cover and cook on Low 10 to 18 hours or on High 4 to 5 hours, stirring occasionally. Stir well during last hour.

Makes 6 to 8 servings

MINESTRONE SOUP

2 packages (16 ounces each)
    frozen vegetables and pasta
    in garlic seasoned sauce
4 cups reduced-sodium vegetable
    juice cocktail
2 cans (15½ ounces each) red
    kidney beans, rinsed and
    drained
1 cup beef broth
1 tablespoon minced onion
½ teaspoon dried Italian
    seasoning
½ teaspoon dried basil leaves
½ teaspoon salt
½ teaspoon black pepper

Combine all ingredients in CROCK-POT® Slow Cooker. Cover and cook on Low 4 to 6 hours or High 2 to 3 hours. Serve.

Makes 8 servings

BLACK BEAN AND POTATO SOUP

6 cups beef broth
1 can (16 ounces) black beans, drained
2 potatoes, diced
½ pound cooked ham, cut into pieces
1 can (4 ounces) chopped jalapeño peppers or mild chili peppers
¼ cup dried chopped onions
1 clove garlic, minced
1 teaspoon ground cumin
1 teaspoon ground oregano leaves
1 teaspoon ground thyme leaves
⅛ teaspoon ground cloves
Sour cream and chopped tomatoes for garnish

In CROCK-POT® Slow Cooker, combine beef broth, beans, potatoes, ham, peppers, onions, garlic, cumin, oregano, thyme and cloves. Cover and cook on Low 8 to 10 hours or on High 4 to 5 hours. Serve. Garnish with sour cream and chopped tomatoes, if desired.   *Makes 6 to 8 servings*

Black Bean and Potato Soup

MINESTRONE ALLA MILANESE

2 cans (14½ ounces each)
   reduced-sodium beef broth
1 can (14½ ounces) diced
   tomatoes, undrained
1 cup diced potato
1 cup coarsely chopped green
   cabbage
1 cup coarsely chopped carrots
1 cup sliced zucchini
¾ cup chopped onion
¾ cup sliced fresh green beans
¾ cup coarsely chopped celery
¾ cup water
2 tablespoons olive oil
1 clove garlic, minced
½ teaspoon dried basil leaves
¼ teaspoon dried rosemary leaves
1 bay leaf
1 can (15½ ounces) cannellini
   beans, rinsed and drained
   Grated Parmesan cheese
   (optional)

Combine all ingredients except cannellini beans and cheese in slow cooker; mix well. Cover and cook on Low 5 to 6 hours. Add cannellini beans. Cover and cook on Low 1 hour or until vegetables are crisp-tender. Remove and discard bay leaf. Garnish with cheese, if desired. *Makes 8 to 10 servings*

Minestrone alla Milanese

SAVORY SOUPS

CLASSIC FRENCH ONION SOUP

¼ cup butter
3 large yellow onions, sliced
1 cup dry white wine
3 cans (about 14 ounces each)
    beef or chicken broth
1 teaspoon Worcestershire sauce
½ teaspoon salt
½ teaspoon dried thyme leaves
1 loaf French bread, sliced
4 ounces shredded Swiss cheese

Melt butter in large skillet over high heat. Add onions; cook and stir 15 minutes or until onions are soft and lightly browned. Stir in wine.

Combine onion mixture, beef broth, Worcestershire, salt and dried thyme in slow cooker. Cover and cook on Low 4 to 4½ hours. Meanwhile, toast bread slices. Ladle soup into 4 individual bowls; top with bread slice and cheese. Garnish with fresh thyme, if desired. *Makes 4 servings*

VEGETABLE CHEESE SOUP

1 can (16 ounces) cream-style corn
1 cup chopped peeled potatoes
1 cup chopped carrots
½ cup chopped onion
1 teaspoon celery seeds
½ teaspoon black pepper
2 cans (14½ ounces each)
    vegetable broth
1 jar (16 ounces) processed cheese

In CROCK-POT® Slow Cooker, combine corn, potatoes, carrots, onion, celery seeds and pepper. Add broth. Cover and cook on Low 8 to 10 hours or on High 4 to 5 hours. If using Low, turn to High. Stir cheese into CROCK-POT® Slow Cooker. Cover and cook 30 to 60 minutes or until cheese is melted and blended. Serve. *Makes 4 to 6 servings*

TIP: Omit potatoes and chopped carrots. Stir in 1 (10-ounce) bag frozen mixed vegetables. Cover and cook on High 2 to 3 hours and then stir in cheese and continue to cook on High until well blended.

Classic French Onion Soup

BEER AND CHEESE SOUP

2 to 3 slices pumpernickel or rye
    bread
1 can (about 14 ounces) chicken
    broth
1 cup beer
¼ cup finely chopped onion
2 cloves garlic, minced
¾ teaspoon dried thyme leaves
6 ounces American cheese,
    shredded or diced
4 to 6 ounces sharp Cheddar
    cheese, shredded
1 cup milk
½ teaspoon paprika

Preheat oven to 425°F. Slice bread into ½-inch cubes; place on baking sheet. Bake 10 to 12 minutes, stirring once, or until crisp; set aside.

Combine chicken broth, beer, onion, garlic and thyme in slow cooker. Cover and cook on Low 4 hours. Turn to High. Stir cheeses, milk and paprika into slow cooker. Cook 45 to 60 minutes or until soup is hot and cheeses are melted. Stir soup well to blend cheeses. Ladle soup into bowls; top with croutons.

Makes 4 (1-cup) servings

Beer and Cheese Soup

RUSSIAN BORSCHT

4 cups thinly sliced green cabbage

1½ pounds fresh beets, shredded

5 small carrots, peeled, cut lengthwise into halves, then cut into 1-inch pieces

1 parsnip, peeled, cut lengthwise into halves, then cut into 1-inch pieces

1 cup chopped onion

4 cloves garlic, minced

1 pound lean beef stew meat, cut into ½-inch cubes

1 can (14½ ounces) diced tomatoes, undrained

3 cans (about 14 ounces each) reduced-sodium beef broth

¼ cup lemon juice

1 tablespoon sugar

1 teaspoon black pepper

Sour cream (optional)

Fresh parsley (optional)

Layer ingredients in slow cooker in following order: cabbage, beets, carrots, parsnip, onion, garlic, beef, tomatoes with juice, broth, lemon juice, sugar and pepper. Cover and cook on Low 7 to 9 hours or until vegetables are crisp-tender. Season with additional lemon juice and sugar, if desired. Dollop with sour cream and garnish with parsley, if desired.   *Makes 12 servings*

Russian Borscht

VEGETABLE AND PASTA SOUP

2 cans (14½ ounces each) beef
    broth
1 can (14 ounces) whole
    tomatoes, undrained
2 zucchini, thinly sliced
1½ cups water
1 onion, chopped
2 carrots, peeled and thinly sliced
2 tablespoons plus 1 teaspoon
    dried parsley flakes
1 tablespoon dried oregano leaves
1½ cups uncooked small
    shell-shaped pasta
    Grated Parmesan cheese

In CROCK-POT® Slow Cooker, combine beef broth, tomatoes, zucchini, water, onion, carrots, parsley and oregano. Cover and cook on Low 8 to 10 hours or High 4 to 5 hours. Stir in uncooked pasta and cook additional 30 minutes or until pasta is tender. Garnish with grated Parmesan cheese. Serve.

Makes 6 to 8 servings

SAVORY SOUPS

BEAN, HAM AND PASTA SOUP

1 cup dried pinto beans, rinsed, drained and picked over
2 tablespoons olive oil
½ pound smoked ham, chopped
1 medium onion, finely chopped
1 medium rib celery, finely chopped
2 cloves garlic, minced
2⅔ cups double strength chicken broth, canned or homemade
3 cups water
¼ cup tomato paste
½ cup spaghetti broken into 1-inch pieces, or bow-tie pasta or shells
¼ teaspoon salt
¼ teaspoon black pepper

In large bowl, combine beans and enough water to cover by 2 inches. Let stand overnight; drain well.

In large skillet, heat oil over medium-high heat. Add ham, onion and celery; cook, stirring often until lightly browned, about 6 minutes. Add garlic and cook, stirring often, 1 minute. Add chicken broth, stirring to scrape up browned bits on bottom of skillet. Transfer to CROCK-POT® Slow Cooker.

Add drained beans, water and tomato paste. Cover and cook until beans are tender, 7 to 8 hours on Low or 4 to 5 hours on High.

Stir in pasta, salt and pepper. Turn to High and cook until pasta is tender, about 30 to 60 minutes.

Using large spoon, crush enough beans against sides of CROCK-POT® Slow Cooker to reach desired consistency. Serve immediately.

Makes 6 to 8 servings

Slow Cooker

STEWS & CHILIES

BEEF BOURGUIGNON

1 boneless beef sirloin steak,
  ½ inch thick, trimmed and
  cut into ½-inch pieces (about
  3 pounds)
½ cup all-purpose flour
4 slices bacon, diced
2 medium carrots, diced
8 small new red potatoes, cut into
  quarters
8 to 10 mushrooms, sliced
20 to 24 fresh pearl onions
3 cloves garlic, minced
1 bay leaf
1 teaspoon dried marjoram
½ teaspoon salt
½ teaspoon dried thyme leaves
  Black pepper to taste
2½ cups Burgundy wine

Coat beef with flour, shaking off excess. Set aside.

Cook bacon in large skillet over medium heat until partially cooked. Add beef; cook until browned. Remove beef and bacon with slotted spoon.

Layer carrots, potatoes, mushrooms, onions, garlic, bay leaf, marjoram, salt, thyme, pepper, beef and bacon mixture and wine in slow cooker. Cover and cook on Low 8 to 9 hours or until beef is tender. Discard bay leaf before serving.

Makes 10 to 12 servings

BACHELOR'S STEW

2 pounds beef chuck, cut into
    1- to 2-inch cubes
$\frac{1}{3}$ cup dry bread crumbs
1 teaspoon salt
$\frac{1}{8}$ teaspoon black pepper
2 cans ($10\frac{3}{4}$ ounces each)
    condensed tomato soup
4 stalks celery, cut into 1-inch
    pieces
3 carrots, peeled, sliced
    lengthwise and cut into
    4-inch strips
1 large onion, cut into eighths
1 cup beef broth or water
1 can (4 ounces) sliced
    mushrooms, undrained
$\frac{1}{3}$ cup quick-cooking tapioca
1 teaspoon dried basil leaves
1 teaspoon Kitchen Bouquet

Dry beef cubes well. Combine bread crumbs, salt and pepper; toss with beef. Place coated beef cubes in CROCK-POT® Slow Cooker and add remaining ingredients; stir well. Cover and cook on Low 10 to 12 hours or on High 3 to 5 hours.

Makes 6 servings

BEEF STEW

2 pounds beef stew meat, cubed
½ cup all-purpose flour
3 tablespoons shortening
1 medium onion, chopped
4 carrots, sliced
3 stalks celery, sliced
1 clove garlic, minced
2 bay leaves
1 teaspoon salt
1 teaspoon sugar
1 teaspoon lemon juice
1 teaspoon Worcestershire sauce
½ teaspoon black pepper
½ teaspoon paprika
⅛ teaspoon ground cloves
4 cups water

Dredge meat in flour; melt shortening in large skillet. Add beef cubes to skillet and sauté until evenly browned. Transfer to CROCK-POT® Slow Cooker. Add onion, carrots, celery, garlic, bay leaves, salt, sugar, lemon juice, Worcestershire sauce, pepper, paprika and cloves. Pour in water and stir. Cover and cook on Low 10 to 12 hours or on High 5 to 6 hours. Remove and discard bay leaves. Serve. *Makes 8 to 10 servings*

MEATBALL STEW

1 pound lean ground beef
1 medium onion, chopped
1 cup dry bread crumbs
1 egg
½ teaspoon salt
¼ teaspoon black pepper
2 tablespoons margarine or butter
1 can (16 ounces) whole
    tomatoes, undrained,
    chopped
1¼ cups water, divided
2 tablespoons beef flavor base
    (paste or granules)
2 teaspoons Italian seasoning
½ teaspoon seasoned salt
¼ teaspoon garlic powder
3 large potatoes, peeled and diced
4 carrots, peeled and sliced
1 medium onion, sliced
2 tablespoons cornstarch

Combine ground beef with chopped onion, bread crumbs, egg, salt and pepper. Shape mixture into about 24 meatballs, then brown in margarine in large skillet; drain well.

Stir together tomatoes, 1 cup water, beef base and seasonings. Place potatoes, carrots and sliced onion in bottom of CROCK-POT® Slow Cooker; top with meatballs. Pour tomato mixture over all. Cover and cook on Low 8 to 10 hours.

Before serving, remove meatballs with slotted spoon. Make smooth paste with cornstarch and remaining ¼ cup water; stir into vegetables. Cover and cook on High 10 minutes to thicken. Return meatballs to stew and serve. *Makes 6 servings*

NABIL'S GRECIAN BEEF STEW

2 pounds lean stewing beef, cut into 1½-inch cubes
2 onions, sliced
2 cloves garlic, chopped
2 tablespoons vegetable oil
1 eggplant, unpeeled, cubed
1 cup beef broth
2½ teaspoons ground cinnamon
1 teaspoon salt
  Black pepper
1 can (16 ounces) garbanzo beans, drained
1 can (16 ounces) tomato wedges, drained
1 tablespoon Kitchen Bouquet
  Hot cooked rice
  Minced parsley

In large skillet, brown beef, onions and garlic in oil; drain. Place in CROCK-POT® Slow Cooker.

Parboil eggplant in 2 cups boiling, salted water for 2 minutes; drain. Add to beef mixture; stir well. Combine beef broth, cinnamon, salt and pepper in small bowl. Pour into CROCK-POT® Slow Cooker; stir well. Cover and cook on Low 10 to 12 hours.

One hour before serving, stir in garbanzo beans, tomato wedges and Kitchen Bouquet. Serve over rice and sprinkle with parsley.

Makes 4 to 6 servings

FRENCH–STYLE PORK STEW

1 tablespoon vegetable oil
1 pork tenderloin (16 ounces), cut into ¾- to 1-inch cubes
1 medium onion, coarsely chopped
1 rib celery, sliced
½ teaspoon dried basil leaves
¼ teaspoon dried rosemary leaves
¼ teaspoon dried oregano leaves
2 tablespoons all-purpose flour
1 cup chicken broth
½ package (16 ounces) frozen mixed vegetables (carrots, potatoes and peas)
1 jar (4½ ounces) sliced mushrooms, drained
1 package (6.2 ounces) long-grain and wild rice
2 teaspoons lemon juice
⅛ teaspoon ground nutmeg
    Salt and black pepper to taste

Heat oil in large skillet over high heat. Add pork, onion, celery, basil, rosemary and oregano. Cook until pork is browned. Place pork mixture in slow cooker. Stir flour into chicken broth; pour into slow cooker.

Stir in frozen vegetables and mushrooms. Cover and cook on Low 4 hours or until pork is barely pink in center. Prepare rice according to package directions, discarding spice packet, if desired.

Stir lemon juice, nutmeg, salt and pepper into slow cooker. Cover and cook 15 minutes. Serve stew over rice.

Makes 4 (1-cup) servings

French-Style Pork Stew

PORK, POTATO AND GREEN BEAN STEW

1 pound boneless pork loin, trimmed of fat and cut into pieces
4 red potatoes, cut into ½-inch cubes
1 onion, chopped
2 cloves garlic, minced
2 cans (14½ ounces each) chicken broth, divided
⅓ cup all-purpose flour
2 cups frozen cut green beans
2 teaspoons Worcestershire sauce
½ teaspoon dried thyme leaves
½ teaspoon black pepper

Heat pork loin, potatoes, onion and garlic with 1 can chicken broth in skillet for 5 to 10 minutes over medium heat. Transfer to CROCK-POT® Slow Cooker.

Combine ¾ cup chicken broth and flour in small bowl. Set aside.

Add remaining broth, green beans, Worcestershire sauce, thyme and pepper to CROCK-POT® Slow Cooker and stir. Cover and cook 8 to 10 hours on Low or 4 to 5 hours on High. If on Low, turn to High last 30 minutes. Stir in flour mixture. Cook 30 minutes to thicken. Serve. *Makes 8 servings*

Pork, Potato and Green Bean Stew

PORK STEW

2 tablespoons vegetable oil,
    divided
3 pounds fresh lean boneless pork
    butt, cut into 1½-inch cubes
2 medium white onions, thinly
    sliced
3 cloves garlic, minced
1 teaspoon salt
1 teaspoon ground cumin
¾ teaspoon dried oregano leaves
1 can (8 ounces) tomatillos,
    drained and chopped *or* 1 cup
    husked and chopped fresh
    tomatillos
1 can (4 ounces) chopped green
    chilies, drained
½ cup reduced-sodium chicken
    broth
1 large tomato, peeled and
    coarsely chopped
¼ cup fresh cilantro, chopped *or*
    ½ teaspoon ground coriander
2 teaspoons lime juice
4 cups hot cooked white rice
½ cup toasted slivered almonds
    (optional)

Heat 1 tablespoon oil in large skillet over medium heat. Add pork; cook 10 minutes or until browned on all sides. Remove and set aside. Heat remaining 1 tablespoon oil in same skillet. Add onions, garlic, salt, cumin and oregano; cook and stir 2 minutes or until soft.

Combine pork, onion mixture and remaining ingredients except rice and almonds in slow cooker; mix well. Cover and cook on Low 5 hours or until pork is tender and barely pink in center. Serve over rice and sprinkle with almonds, if desired.

Makes 10 servings

Pork Stew

ITALIAN SAUSAGE AND VEGETABLE STEW

1 pound hot or mild Italian
    sausage, cut into 1-inch pieces
1 package (16 ounces) frozen
    mixed vegetables (onions and
    green, red and yellow bell
    peppers)
1 can (14½ ounces) diced
    Italian-style tomatoes,
    undrained
2 medium zucchini, sliced
1 jar (4½ ounces) sliced
    mushrooms, drained
4 cloves garlic, minced
2 tablespoons Italian-style tomato
    paste

Heat large skillet over high heat until hot. Add sausage; cook about 5 minutes or until browned. Pour off any drippings.

Combine sausage, frozen vegetables, tomatoes, zucchini, mushrooms and garlic in slow cooker. Cover and cook on Low 4 to 4½ hours or until zucchini is tender. Stir in tomato paste. Cover and cook 30 minutes or until juices have thickened.

Makes 6 (1-cup) servings

SERVING SUGGESTION: Serve with fresh hot garlic bread.

Italian Sausage and Vegetable Stew

LAMB IN DILL SAUCE

2 large boiling potatoes, peeled
and cut into 1-inch cubes
½ cup chopped onion
1½ teaspoons salt
½ teaspoon black pepper
½ teaspoon dried dill weed *or*
4 sprigs fresh dill
1 bay leaf
2 pounds lean lamb stew meat,
cut into 1-inch cubes
1 cup plus 3 tablespoons water,
divided
2 tablespoons all-purpose flour
1 teaspoon sugar
2 tablespoons lemon juice
Fresh dill (optional)

Layer ingredients in slow cooker in following order: potatoes, onion, salt, pepper, dill, bay leaf, lamb and 1 cup water. Cover and cook on Low 6 to 8 hours.

Remove lamb and potatoes with slotted spoon; cover and keep warm. Remove and discard bay leaf. Turn heat to High. Stir flour and remaining 3 tablespoons water in small bowl until smooth. Add half of cooking juices and sugar. Mix well and return to slow cooker. Cover and cook 15 minutes. Stir in lemon juice. Return lamb and potatoes to slow cooker. Cover and cook 10 minutes or until heated through. Garnish with fresh dill, if desired.
Makes 6 servings

Lamb in Dill Sauce

CHICKEN STEW WITH DUMPLINGS

2 cups sliced carrots
1 cup chopped onion
1 large green bell pepper, sliced
½ cup sliced celery
2 cans (about 14 ounces each) chicken broth
⅔ cup all-purpose flour
1 pound boneless skinless chicken breasts, cut into 1-inch pieces
1 potato, unpeeled, diced
6 ounces mushrooms, halved
¾ cup frozen peas
1 teaspoon dried basil leaves
¾ teaspoon dried rosemary
¼ teaspoon dried tarragon
¼ cup heavy cream
¾ to 1 teaspoon salt
¼ teaspoon black pepper

HERB DUMPLINGS

1 cup biscuit mix
¼ teaspoon dried basil leaves
¼ teaspoon dried rosemary
⅛ teaspoon dried tarragon
⅓ cup reduced-fat (2%) milk

Combine carrots, onion, bell pepper and celery in slow cooker. Stir in chicken broth, reserving 1 cup broth. Cover and cook on Low 2 hours.

Stir flour into remaining 1 cup broth until smooth. Stir into slow cooker. Add chicken, potato, mushrooms, peas and herbs to slow cooker. Cover and cook 4 hours or until vegetables are tender and chicken is no longer pink. Stir in cream, salt and black pepper.

For Herb Dumplings, combine biscuit mix and herbs in small bowl. Stir in milk to form soft dough. Spoon dumpling mixture on top of stew in 4 large spoonfuls. Cook, uncovered, 30 minutes. Cover and cook 30 to 45 minutes or until dumplings are firm and toothpick inserted in center comes out clean. Serve in shallow bowls. *Makes 4 servings*

Chicken Stew with Dumplings

CHINESE CHICKEN STEW

1 pound boneless skinless chicken thighs, cut into 1-inch pieces

1 teaspoon Chinese five-spice powder

½ to ¾ teaspoon red pepper flakes

1 tablespoon peanut or vegetable oil

1 large onion, coarsely chopped

1 package (8 ounces) fresh mushrooms, sliced

2 cloves garlic, minced

1 can (about 14 ounces) chicken broth, divided

1 tablespoon cornstarch

1 large red bell pepper, cut into ¾-inch pieces

2 tablespoons soy sauce

1 tablespoon sesame oil

2 large green onions, cut into ½-inch pieces

3 cups hot cooked white rice (optional)

¼ cup coarsely chopped cilantro (optional)

Toss chicken with five-spice powder in small bowl. Season with red pepper flakes. Heat peanut oil in large skillet. Add onion and chicken; cook and stir about 5 minutes or until chicken is browned. Add mushrooms and garlic; cook and stir until chicken is no longer pink.

Combine ¼ cup broth and cornstarch in small bowl; set aside. Place cooked chicken mixture, remaining broth, bell pepper and soy sauce in slow cooker. Cover and cook on Low 3½ hours or until bell pepper is tender.

Stir in cornstarch mixture, sesame oil and green onions; cook 30 to 45 minutes or until juices have thickened. Ladle into soup bowls; scoop ½ cup rice into each bowl. Sprinkle with cilantro, if desired.   *Makes 6 servings (about 5 cups)*

Chinese Chicken Stew

GREEK–STYLE CHICKEN STEW

2 cups cubed peeled eggplant
2 cups sliced mushrooms
1¼ cups low-sodium chicken broth
¾ cup coarsely chopped onion
2 cloves garlic, minced
1½ teaspoons all-purpose flour
1 teaspoon dried oregano leaves
½ teaspoon dried basil leaves
½ teaspoon dried thyme leaves
6 skinless chicken breasts, about
    2 pounds
    Additional all-purpose flour
3 tablespoons dry sherry or
    low-sodium chicken broth
¼ teaspoon salt
¼ teaspoon black pepper
1 can (14 ounces) artichoke
    hearts, drained
12 ounces uncooked wide egg
    noodles

Combine eggplant, mushrooms, broth, onion, garlic, 1½ teaspoons flour, oregano, basil and thyme in slow cooker. Cover and cook on High 1 hour.

Coat chicken very lightly with additional flour. Generously spray large nonstick skillet with cooking spray; heat over medium heat until hot. Cook chicken 10 to 15 minutes or until browned on all sides.

Remove vegetables to bowl with slotted spoon. Layer chicken in slow cooker; return vegetables to slow cooker. Add sherry, salt and pepper. Reduce heat to Low; cover and cook 6 to 6½ hours or until chicken is no longer pink in center and vegetables are tender.

Stir in artichokes; cover and cook 45 minutes to 1 hour or until heated through. Cook noodles according to package directions. Serve chicken stew over noodles. *Makes 6 servings*

Greek-Style Chicken Stew

TURKEY MUSHROOM STEW

1 pound turkey cutlets, cut into
   4×1-inch strips
1 small onion, thinly sliced
2 tablespoons minced green
   onions with tops
½ pound mushrooms, sliced
2 to 3 tablespoons all-purpose
   flour
1 cup half-and-half or milk
1 teaspoon dried tarragon leaves
1 teaspoon salt
   Black pepper to taste
½ cup frozen peas
½ cup sour cream (optional)
   Puff pastry shells (optional)

Layer turkey, onions and mushrooms in slow cooker. Cover and cook on Low 4 hours. Remove turkey and vegetables to serving bowl. Turn slow cooker to High.

Blend flour into half-and-half until smooth; pour into slow cooker. Add tarragon, salt and pepper to slow cooker. Return cooked vegetables and turkey to slow cooker. Stir in peas. Cover and cook 1 hour or until sauce has thickened and peas are heated through.

Stir in sour cream just before serving for a richer flavor. Serve in puff pastry shells, if desired. *Makes 4 servings*

Turkey Mushroom Stew

SOUTHWEST TURKEY TENDERLOIN STEW

1 package (about 1½ pounds)
    turkey tenderloins, cut into
    ¾-inch pieces
1 tablespoon chili powder
1 teaspoon ground cumin
¾ teaspoon salt
1 can (15½ ounces) chili beans in
    spicy sauce, undrained
1 can (14½ ounces) chili-style
    stewed tomatoes, undrained
1 red bell pepper, cut into ¾-inch
    pieces
1 green bell pepper, cut into
    ¾-inch pieces
¾ cup chopped red or yellow onion
¾ cup prepared salsa or picante
    sauce
3 cloves garlic, minced
  Fresh cilantro (optional)

Place turkey in slow cooker. Sprinkle chili powder, cumin and salt over turkey; toss to coat. Add beans, tomatoes, bell peppers, onion, salsa and garlic. Mix well. Cover and cook on Low 5 hours or until turkey is no longer pink in center and vegetables are crisp-tender. Ladle into bowls. Garnish with cilantro, if desired.
Makes 6 servings

Southwest Turkey Tenderloin Stew

GARDEN VEGETABLE TABBOULEH STEW

1 large onion, chopped
2 medium carrots, cut lengthwise into halves, then cut into 1-inch pieces
1 cup green beans, cut into 1-inch pieces
2 medium green onions, thinly sliced
1 small zucchini (4 ounces), sliced
1 can (15½ ounces) chick-peas (garbanzo beans), rinsed and drained
2 cans (14½ ounces each) diced tomatoes, undrained
¼ teaspoon salt
⅛ teaspoon black pepper
1 box (6 to 7 ounces) tabbouleh mix
1½ cups water
¼ cup olive oil
   Sour cream (optional)
   Fresh mint (optional)

Layer ingredients in slow cooker in following order: onion, carrots, green beans, green onions, zucchini, chick-peas, tomatoes with juice, salt and pepper. Sprinkle tabbouleh mix over vegetables. Pour water and olive oil evenly over top. Cover and cook on Low 6 to 8 hours or until vegetables are crisp-tender. Serve in bowls and garnish with sour cream and fresh mint, if desired.

Makes 4 servings

Garden Vegetable Tabbouleh Stew

LENTIL STEW OVER COUSCOUS

3 cups lentils (1 pound), rinsed

3 cups water

1 can (14½ ounces) diced tomatoes, undrained

1 can (14½ ounces) reduced-sodium chicken broth

4 ribs celery, chopped

1 large onion, chopped

1 green bell pepper, chopped

1 medium carrot, cut lengthwise into halves, then cut into 1-inch pieces

2 cloves garlic, chopped

1 teaspoon dried marjoram leaves

¼ teaspoon black pepper

1 tablespoon cider vinegar

1 tablespoon olive oil

4½ to 5 cups hot cooked couscous

Carrot curls (optional)

Celery leaves (optional)

Combine lentils, water, tomatoes, broth, celery, onion, bell pepper, carrot, garlic, marjoram and black pepper in slow cooker. Stir; cover and cook on Low 8 to 9 hours.

Stir in vinegar and olive oil. Serve over couscous. Garnish with carrot curls and celery leaves, if desired. *Makes 12 servings*

TIP: Lentil stew keeps well in the refrigerator for up to one week. Stew can also be frozen in airtight container in freezer up to three months.

Lentil Stew over Couscous

MIDDLE EASTERN VEGETABLE STEW

1 can (28 ounces) crushed
    tomatoes in purée
3 cups (12 ounces) sliced zucchini
2 cups (6 ounces) cubed peeled
    eggplant
2 cups (8 ounces) sliced
    quartered sweet potatoes
1½ cups cubed peeled butternut
    squash
1 cup drained garbanzo beans
½ cup raisins or currants
1 tablespoon olive oil
1½ teaspoons ground cinnamon
1 teaspoon grated orange peel
¾ to 1 teaspoon ground cumin
½ teaspoon salt
½ teaspoon paprika
¼ to ½ teaspoon ground red
    pepper
⅛ teaspoon ground cardamom
   Hot cooked rice or couscous
    (optional)

Combine all ingredients except rice in slow cooker. Cover and cook on Low 5 to 5½ hours or until vegetables are tender. Serve over rice.

Makes 4 to 6 servings

SAVORY BEAN STEW

1 can (15½ ounces) chick-peas, rinsed and drained

1 can (15 ounces) pinto beans, rinsed and drained

1 can (15 ounces) black beans, rinsed and drained

1 can (14½ ounces) diced tomatoes with roasted garlic, undrained

1 cup frozen vegetable seasoning blend (onions, celery, red and green bell peppers)

¾ teaspoon dried thyme leaves

¾ teaspoon dried sage leaves

½ to ¾ teaspoon dried oregano leaves

1 tablespoon all-purpose flour

¾ cup vegetable or chicken broth, divided

POLENTA

3 cups water

¾ cup yellow cornmeal

¾ teaspoon salt

Additional salt and black pepper to taste

Combine chick-peas, beans, tomatoes with juice, frozen vegetable blend and herbs in slow cooker. Stir flour into ½ cup vegetable broth; pour into bean mixture and stir well. Cover and cook on Low 4 hours or until vegetables are tender and juice is thickened.

Meanwhile, prepare polenta. Bring water to a boil in large saucepan. Reduce heat; gradually stir in cornmeal and ¾ teaspoon salt. Cook 5 to 8 minutes or until cornmeal thickens. Season to taste with additional salt and pepper. Keep warm.

Stir remaining ¼ cup broth into slow cooker. Spread polenta on plate and top with stew. *Makes 6 (1-cup) servings*

MEDITERRANEAN STEW

1 medium butternut or acorn
    squash, peeled and cut into
    1-inch cubes
2 cups unpeeled eggplant cut into
    1-inch cubes
2 cups sliced zucchini
1 can (15½ ounces) chick-peas,
    rinsed and drained
1 package (10 ounces) frozen cut
    okra
1 can (8 ounces) tomato sauce
1 cup chopped onion
1 medium tomato, chopped
1 medium carrot, thinly sliced
½ cup reduced-sodium vegetable
    broth
⅓ cup raisins
1 clove garlic, minced
½ teaspoon ground cumin
½ teaspoon ground turmeric
¼ to ½ teaspoon ground red
    pepper
¼ teaspoon ground cinnamon
¼ teaspoon paprika
6 to 8 cups hot cooked couscous
    or rice

Combine all ingredients, except couscous, in slow cooker; mix well. Cover and cook on Low 8 to 10 hours or until vegetables are crisp-tender. Serve over couscous. Garnish with parsley, if desired.

Makes 6 servings

Mediterranean Stew

BEAN RAGOÛT WITH CILANTRO–CORNMEAL DUMPLINGS

1 can (15½ ounces) *each* pinto and black beans, rinsed and drained

2 cans (14½ ounces each) diced tomatoes, undrained

1½ cups chopped red bell pepper

2 small zucchini, sliced

1 large onion, chopped

½ cup chopped green bell pepper

½ cup chopped celery

1 poblano chili pepper, chopped

2 cloves garlic, minced

3 tablespoons chili powder

2 teaspoons ground cumin

1 teaspoon dried oregano leaves

½ teaspoon salt, divided

⅛ teaspoon black pepper

¼ cup all-purpose flour

¼ cup yellow cornmeal

½ teaspoon baking powder

1 tablespoon vegetable shortening

2 tablespoons shredded Cheddar cheese

2 teaspoons minced fresh cilantro

¼ cup milk

Combine beans, tomatoes with juice, red bell pepper, zucchini, onion, green bell pepper, celery, poblano pepper, garlic, chili powder, cumin, oregano, ¼ teaspoon salt and black pepper in slow cooker; mix well. Cover and cook on Low 7 to 8 hours.

Prepare dumplings 1 hour before serving. Mix flour, cornmeal, baking powder and remaining ¼ teaspoon salt in medium bowl. Cut in shortening with pastry blender or two knives until mixture resembles coarse crumbs. Stir in cheese and cilantro. Pour milk into flour mixture. Blend just until dry ingredients are moistened. Turn slow cooker to High. Drop dumplings by level tablespoonfuls (larger dumplings will not cook properly) on top of ragoût. Cover and cook 1 hour or until toothpick inserted in dumpling comes out clean. *Makes 6 servings*

Bean Ragoût with Cilantro-Cornmeal Dumplings

SOUTHWEST BEAN CHILI

1 can (16 ounces) tomato sauce
1 can (15 ounces) garbanzo
  beans, rinsed and drained
1 can (15 ounces) red kidney
  beans, rinsed and drained
1 can (15 ounces) black beans,
  rinsed and drained
1 can (14½ ounces) Mexican-style
  stewed tomatoes, undrained
1½ cups frozen corn
2 medium green bell peppers,
  seeded and chopped
1 cup chicken broth
3 tablespoons chili powder
4 cloves garlic, minced
1 tablespoon cocoa powder
1 teaspoon ground cumin
½ teaspoon salt
  Hot cooked rice

TOPPINGS
  Shredded cheese, ripe olives,
    avocado and green onion
    slices (optional)

Combine all ingredients except rice and toppings in slow cooker. Cover and cook on Low 6 to 6½ hours or until vegetables are tender.

Spoon rice into bowls; top with chili. Serve with toppings, if desired.
Makes 8 to 10 servings

Southwest Bean Chili

TURKEY VEGETABLE CHILI MAC

¾ pound ground turkey breast
1 can (about 15 ounces) black
    beans, rinsed and drained
1 can (14½ ounces) Mexican-style
    stewed tomatoes, undrained
1 can (14½ ounces) no-salt-added
    diced tomatoes, undrained
1 cup frozen corn
½ cup chopped onion
2 cloves garlic, minced
1 teaspoon Mexican seasoning
½ cup uncooked elbow macaroni
⅓ cup sour cream

Spray large skillet with nonstick cooking spray. Add turkey; cook until browned. Combine cooked turkey, beans, tomatoes with juice, corn, onion, garlic and seasoning in slow cooker. Cover and cook on Low 4 to 5 hours.

Stir in macaroni. Cover and cook 10 minutes; stir. Cover and cook 20 to 30 minutes or until pasta is tender. Serve with sour cream.

Makes 6 servings

FIVE-ALARM BEEF CHILI

¼ cup vegetable oil or olive oil, divided
3 to 4 pounds boneless beef chuck, cut into pieces
2 onions, chopped
2 green bell peppers, chopped
1 cup beer
1 can (4 ounces) chopped jalapeño or mild chili peppers
⅓ cup chili powder
1 tablespoon dried oregano
2 teaspoons ground cumin
1 teaspoon salt

Heat 2 tablespoons oil in skillet over medium heat. Add beef and brown all sides. Transfer to CROCK-POT® Slow Cooker. Add remaining 2 tablespoons oil to skillet and sauté onions and bell peppers until soft. Transfer to CROCK-POT® Slow Cooker. In CROCK-POT® Slow Cooker, stir in beer, jalapeños, chili powder, oregano, cumin and salt. Cover and cook on Low 6 to 8 hours or on High 3 to 4 hours. Serve. *Makes 6 to 8 servings*

CHUNKY CHILI

1 pound lean ground beef
1 medium onion, chopped
2 cans (16 ounces each) diced
    tomatoes, undrained
1 can (15 ounces) pinto beans,
    rinsed and drained
½ cup prepared salsa
1 tablespoon chili powder
1½ teaspoons ground cumin
    Salt and black pepper to taste
½ cup (2 ounces) shredded
    Cheddar cheese
3 tablespoons sour cream
4 teaspoons sliced black olives

Heat large skillet over medium heat. Add beef and onion; cook until beef is browned and onion is tender. Drain fat. Place beef mixture, tomatoes, beans, salsa, chili powder and cumin in slow cooker; stir. Cover and cook on Low 5 to 6 hours or until flavors are blended and chili is bubbly. Season with salt and pepper to taste. Serve with cheese, sour cream and olives.

Makes 4 (1½-cup) servings

SERVING SUGGESTION: Serve with tossed green salad and cornbread muffins.

Chunky Chili

VEGETABLE CHILI

1 can (28 ounces) whole
    tomatoes, undrained
1 can (16 ounces) garbanzo
    beans, drained
2 zucchini, thinly sliced
1 large onion, chopped
2 carrots, thinly sliced
2 ribs celery, thinly sliced
1 red bell pepper, seeded and
    chopped
1 green bell pepper, seeded and
    chopped
1 can (4 ounces) chopped green
    chilies
⅓ cup chili powder
2 cloves garlic, minced
1 tablespoon dried oregano leaves
2 teaspoons ground cumin
1 teaspoon salt
    Sour cream for garnish

In CROCK-POT® Slow Cooker, combine tomatoes, beans, zucchini, onion, carrots, celery, bell peppers, green chilies, chili powder, garlic, oregano, cumin and salt. Cover and cook on Low 6 to 8 hours or on High 3 to 4 hours. Cook until vegetables are tender. Serve immediately. Garnish with sour cream, if desired.

Makes 6 to 8 servings

WHITE BEAN CHILI

1 pound ground chicken
3 cups coarsely chopped celery
1 can (16 ounces) whole tomatoes, undrained, coarsely chopped
1 can (15½ ounces) Great Northern beans, drained and rinsed
1½ cups coarsely chopped onions
1 cup chicken broth
3 cloves garlic, minced
4 teaspoons chili powder
1½ teaspoons ground cumin
¾ teaspoon ground allspice
¾ teaspoon ground cinnamon
½ teaspoon black pepper

Spray large nonstick skillet with cooking spray; heat over high heat until hot. Add chicken; cook until browned, breaking into pieces with fork. Combine chicken, celery, tomatoes, beans, onions, broth, garlic, chili powder, cumin, allspice, cinnamon and pepper in slow cooker. Cover and cook 5½ to 6 hours on Low or until chicken is no longer pink and celery is tender.

Makes 6 servings

TWO–BEAN CORN CHILI

1 can (16 ounces) black-eyed peas
1 can (16 ounces) navy beans
1 onion, chopped
1 cup water
1 cup fresh, frozen or canned corn
1 cup diced tomatoes
½ cup chopped green onions
½ cup tomato paste
¼ cup diced canned jalapeño peppers
2 teaspoons chili powder
1 teaspoon prepared mustard
½ teaspoon ground cumin
¼ teaspoon dried oregano leaves

Combine all ingredients in CROCK-POT® Slow Cooker. Cover and cook on Low 8 to 10 hours or on High 4 to 5 hours. Serve.

Makes 6 to 8 servings

Two-Bean Corn Chili

NO–BEANS BEEF CHILI WITH CORNMEAL

2 pounds ground beef
1 onion, chopped
1 green bell pepper
2 cloves garlic, minced
1 can (10 ounces) enchilada sauce
1 can (8 ounces) tomato sauce
1 can (4½ ounces) chopped black
    olives, drained
2 tablespoons chili powder
1 teaspoon salt
1 teaspoon dried oregano
½ teaspoon ground cumin
2 cups water
1 cup yellow cornmeal
2 cups shredded Cheddar cheese

In skillet over medium heat, cook ground beef, onion, bell pepper and garlic until meat browns. Drain fat. Transfer to CROCK-POT® Slow Cooker. Stir in enchilada sauce, tomato sauce, olives, chili powder, salt, oregano and cumin. Cover and cook on Low 8 to 10 hours or on High 4 to 5 hours.

In saucepan, bring water to a boil and gradually stir in cornmeal. Reduce heat to low and cook until thick. Drop cornmeal by tablespoonfuls onto chili. Increase heat to High if cooking on Low. Cover and cook 20 to 25 minutes. Sprinkle cornmeal with cheese and cook until cheese is melted. Serve.

Makes 6 to 8 servings

CHILI VERDE

¾ pound boneless lean pork, cut
   into 1-inch cubes
1 pound fresh tomatillos, coarsely
   chopped
1 can (15 ounces) Great Northern
   beans, rinsed and drained
1 can (about 14 ounces) chicken
   broth
1 large onion, halved and thinly
   sliced
1 can (4 ounces) diced mild green
   chilies
6 cloves garlic, chopped or sliced
1 teaspoon ground cumin
   Salt and black pepper to taste
½ cup lightly packed fresh
   cilantro, chopped
   Sour cream

Spray large skillet with nonstick cooking spray and heat over medium-high heat. Add pork; cook until browned on all sides.

Combine cooked pork and all remaining ingredients except cilantro and sour cream in slow cooker. Cover and cook on High 3 to 4 hours. Season with salt and pepper. Gently press meat against side of slow cooker with wooden spoon to shred. Reduce heat to Low. Stir in cilantro and cook 10 minutes. Serve with sour cream. *Makes 4 servings*

Slow Cooker

MAIN DISHES

CHICKEN IN WINE

3 pounds chicken pieces,
    preferably breasts and thighs
Salt and black pepper
2 tablespoons butter
1 medium onion, sliced
1 can (4 ounces) sliced
    mushrooms, drained
½ cup dry sherry
1 teaspoon Italian seasoning
Hot cooked rice

Rinse chicken parts and pat dry. Season chicken lightly with salt and pepper. In skillet, melt butter and quickly brown chicken parts; remove with slotted spoon and place in CROCK-POT® Slow Cooker. Sauté onion and mushrooms in skillet. Add sherry to skillet and stir, scraping to remove brown particles. Pour contents of skillet into CROCK-POT® Slow Cooker over chicken. Sprinkle with Italian seasoning. Cover and cook on Low 8 to 10 hours or on High 3 to 4 hours.

Serve chicken over rice and spoon sauce over top.

Makes 4 to 6 servings

CHICKEN BREASTS À L'ORANGE

3 whole chicken breasts, cut into halves
⅔ cup plus 3 tablespoons all-purpose flour, divided
1 teaspoon salt
1 teaspoon ground nutmeg
½ teaspoon ground cinnamon
Dash black pepper
Dash garlic powder
2 to 3 sweet potatoes, peeled and cut into ¼-inch slices
1 can (10¾ ounces) condensed cream of celery or cream of chicken soup
1 can (4 ounces) sliced mushrooms, drained
½ cup orange juice
2 teaspoons brown sugar
½ teaspoon grated orange peel
Hot buttered rice

Rinse chicken breasts and pat dry. Combine ⅔ cup flour with salt, nutmeg, cinnamon, pepper and garlic powder. Thoroughly coat chicken in flour mixture.

Place sweet potato slices in bottom of CROCK-POT® Slow Cooker. Place chicken breasts on top.

Combine soup with mushrooms, orange juice, brown sugar, orange peel and remaining 3 tablespoons flour; stir well. Pour soup mixture over chicken breasts. Cover and cook on Low 8 to 10 hours or on High 3 to 4 hours or until chicken and vegetables are tender.

Serve chicken and sauce over hot buttered rice.

Make 6 servings

Chicken Breasts à l'Orange

BAKED CHICKEN BREASTS

2 to 3 whole chicken breasts, cut
 into halves
1 can (10¾ ounces) condensed
 cream of chicken soup
½ cup dry sherry
1 can (4 ounces) sliced
 mushrooms, drained
2 tablespoons butter or
 margarine, melted
1 teaspoon Worcestershire sauce
1 teaspoon dried tarragon leaves
 or dried rosemary
¼ teaspoon garlic powder

Rinse chicken breasts and pat dry; place in CROCK-POT® Slow Cooker. Combine remaining ingredients and pour over chicken breasts. Cover and cook on Low 8 to 10 hours or on High 4 to 5 hours.

Makes 4 to 6 servings

CREAMY CHICKEN AND HAM MEDLEY

$\frac{1}{3}$ cup margarine or butter
$\frac{1}{3}$ cup all-purpose flour
2$\frac{1}{2}$ cups milk
2 cups chopped cooked chicken
2 cups chopped cooked ham
1 cup grated Parmesan cheese
1 can (4 ounces) sliced
    mushrooms, drained
$\frac{1}{2}$ teaspoon salt
$\frac{1}{4}$ teaspoon black pepper
$\frac{1}{4}$ teaspoon ground nutmeg
    Dash ground red pepper
2 packages (10 ounces each)
    frozen puff pastry shells,
    baked
    Paprika

Melt margarine in CROCK-POT® Slow Cooker; stir in flour. Stir in remaining ingredients except pastry shells and paprika. Cook on Low 2$\frac{1}{2}$ hours until thickened, stirring after every hour.

Bake pastry shells as directed on package. Spoon chicken and ham medley into pastry shells and sprinkle with paprika. Serve immediately.   *Makes 4 to 6 servings*

CHICKEN CURRY

**2 boneless skinless chicken breast
    halves, cut into ¾-inch pieces**
**1 cup coarsely chopped apple,
    divided**
1 small onion, sliced
3 tablespoons raisins
1 teaspoon curry powder
1 clove garlic, minced
¼ teaspoon ground ginger
⅓ cup water
**1½ teaspoons chicken bouillon
    granules**
1½ teaspoons all-purpose flour
¼ cup sour cream
½ teaspoon cornstarch
½ cup uncooked white rice

Combine chicken, ¾ cup apple, onion, raisins, curry powder, garlic and ginger in slow cooker. Combine water, chicken bouillon granules and flour in small bowl; stir until dissolved. Add to slow cooker. Cover and cook on Low 3½ to 4 hours or until onions are tender and chicken is no longer pink.

Combine sour cream and cornstarch in large bowl. Turn off slow cooker; remove insert to heatproof surface. Drain all cooking liquid from chicken mixture and stir into sour cream mixture. Add back to insert; stir well. Place insert back in slow cooker. Cover and let stand 5 to 10 minutes or until sauce is heated through.

Meanwhile, cook rice according to package directions. Serve chicken curry over rice; garnish with remaining ¼ cup apple.

Makes 2 servings

TIP: For a special touch, sprinkle chicken with green onion slivers just before serving.

Chicken Curry

CHICKEN CHOW MEIN

1 (4-pound) hen or fryer chicken,
 cut up
2 cups water
2 large white onions, chopped
2 cups diagonally sliced celery
¼ cup all-purpose flour or
 cornstarch
¼ cup soy sauce
1 can (16 ounces) bean sprouts,
 drained
1 can (6 or 8½ ounces) water
 chestnuts, drained and sliced
1 can (5 or 6 ounces) bamboo
 shoots (optional)
3 tablespoons molasses
 Chow mein noodles or hot rice
 Toasted slivered almonds

Place chicken, water, onions and celery in CROCK-POT® Slow Cooker. Cover and cook on Low for 8 to 10 hours.

One hour before serving, turn to High. Remove chicken; bone and cut up meat into bite-size pieces. Return to CROCK-POT® Slow Cooker. Combine flour and soy sauce; stir into CROCK-POT® Slow Cooker with bean sprouts, water chestnuts, bamboo shoots and molasses. Stir well until thickened. Taste for seasoning. Turn to Low until ready to serve, up to 4 hours.

Serve over chow mein noodles or hot cooked rice. Sprinkle with toasted slivered almonds. *Makes 8 to 10 servings*

CHICKEN ENCHILADAS

Mexican Gravy (recipe follows)
2 to 3 pounds chopped cooked chicken
1 onion, chopped
1 can (4½ ounces) chopped mild green chilies
8 corn tortillas
1 cup (4 ounces) shredded Monterey Jack cheese
1 cup (4 ounces) shredded mild or sharp Cheddar cheese
1 can (4 ounces) chopped black olives

Prepare Mexican Gravy. In mixing bowl, stir together chicken, onion, chilies and 1 cup Mexican Gravy.

In CROCK-POT® Slow Cooker, place foil handles (see page 7). Dip 1 tortilla in Mexican Gravy and lay in CROCK-POT® Slow Cooker. Spread about 3 tablespoons chicken filling over tortilla and sprinkle with ⅛ of cheeses and olives. Continue layering process until top of CROCK-POT® Slow Cooker has been reached. Final layer should be cheese and olive layer. Pour any excess gravy over top of tortilla stack. Cook on Low 4 to 6 hours or on High 1½ to 2½ hours. *Makes 6 to 8 servings*

MEXICAN GRAVY

¼ cup (½ stick) margarine or butter
½ cup chili powder
⅓ cup all-purpose flour
½ teaspoon garlic salt
¼ teaspoon ground cumin
¼ teaspoon dried oregano leaves
3 cans (15 ounces each) chicken broth
1 can (12 ounces) tomato sauce

Melt margarine in saucepan. In bowl, mix together dry ingredients. Slowly add chili powder, flour, salt, cumin and oregano to margarine, stirring constantly. Mixture will become crumbly. Slowly add chicken broth to margarine mixture, stirring constantly. Stir in tomato sauce. *Makes about 2 quarts*

MAIN DISHES

ALMOND CHICKEN

1 can (14 ounces) chicken broth
1 slice bacon, diced
2 tablespoons butter
¾ to 1 pound boneless chicken
    breasts, cut into 1-inch pieces
1½ cups diagonally sliced celery
1 small onion, sliced
1 can (4 ounces) sliced
    mushrooms, drained
2 tablespoons soy sauce
½ teaspoon salt
    Hot cooked rice
⅔ cup slivered almonds, toasted

Pour chicken broth into CROCK-POT® Slow Cooker. Cover and turn CROCK-POT® Slow Cooker to High.

In large skillet, heat bacon and butter; add chicken pieces and brown quickly on all sides. With slotted spoon, remove browned chicken to CROCK-POT® Slow Cooker. Quickly sauté celery, onion and mushrooms in skillet until just slightly limp.

Add contents of skillet to CROCK-POT® Slow Cooker with soy sauce and salt; stir well. Cover and cook on Low 6 to 8 hours or on High 3 to 4 hours.

Serve over hot fluffy rice and garnish with toasted almonds.

Makes 4 servings

SWISS CHICKEN CASSEROLE

6 boneless skinless chicken
    breasts
6 slices (4×4-inch) Swiss cheese
1 can (10¾ ounces) cream of
    mushroom soup, undiluted
¼ cup milk
2 cups herb stuffing mix
½ cup margarine or butter, melted

Spray CROCK-POT® Slow Cooker with cooking spray. Arrange chicken breasts in CROCK-POT® Slow Cooker. Top with cheese, layering cheese if necessary. Combine soup and milk; stir well. Spoon over cheese; sprinkle with stuffing mix. Drizzle melted margarine over stuffing mix. Cook on Low 8 to 10 hours or on High 4 to 6 hours.

Makes 6 servings

CHICKEN FRICASSEE

1 (3- to 4-pound) stewing chicken or fryer, cut into serving pieces
2 teaspoons salt
1 teaspoon paprika
2 medium onions, sliced
3 stalks celery, sliced
2 carrots, peeled and sliced
1 bay leaf
1 cup chicken broth
½ cup all-purpose flour
½ cup water
1 package (10 ounces) noodles, cooked and drained
Chopped parsley

Rinse chicken and pat dry. Season with salt and paprika. Place onions, celery, carrots and bay leaf in CROCK-POT® Slow Cooker. Place chicken pieces on top of vegetables. Pour in chicken broth. Cover and cook on Low 8 to 12 hours or on High 4 to 6 hours. Remove bay leaf.

One hour before serving, turn to High. Remove chicken pieces; bone and return meat to CROCK-POT® Slow Cooker. Make smooth paste of flour and water and stir into liquid in CROCK-POT® Slow Cooker. Cover and cook until thickened.

Serve over hot noodles; sprinkle with chopped parsley.

Makes 6 to 8 servings

COMPANY CHICKEN CASSEROLE

1 package (8 ounces) noodles
3 cups diced cooked chicken
1½ cups cream-style cottage cheese
1 can (10¾ ounces) condensed cream of chicken soup
1 cup grated sharp processed cheese
½ cup diced celery
½ cup diced green bell pepper
½ cup diced onion
1 can (4 ounces) sliced mushrooms, drained
1 jar (4 ounces) pimientos, diced
½ cup grated Parmesan cheese
½ cup chicken broth
2 tablespoons butter, melted
½ teaspoon dried basil leaves

Cook noodles according to package directions in boiling water until barely tender; drain and rinse thoroughly. In large bowl, combine remaining ingredients with noodles, making certain noodles are separated and coated with liquid. Pour mixture into greased CROCK-POT® Slow Cooker. Cover and cook on Low 6 to 10 hours or on High 3 to 4 hours. *Makes 6 servings*

COMPANY TURKEY CASSEROLE: Substitute diced cooked turkey for chicken.

Company Chicken Casserole

COQ AU VIN

4 slices thick-cut bacon

2 cups frozen pearl onions, thawed

1 cup sliced button mushrooms

1 clove garlic, minced

1 teaspoon dried thyme leaves

⅛ teaspoon black pepper

6 boneless skinless chicken breast halves (about 2 pounds)

½ cup dry red wine

¾ cup reduced-sodium chicken broth

¼ cup tomato paste

3 tablespoons all-purpose flour

Cook bacon in medium skillet over medium heat. Drain and crumble. Layer ingredients in slow cooker in the following order: onions, bacon, mushrooms, garlic, thyme, pepper, chicken, wine and broth. Cover and cook on Low 6 to 8 hours.

Remove chicken and vegetables; cover and keep warm. Ladle ½ cup cooking liquid into small bowl; allow to cool slightly. Turn slow cooker to High; cover. Mix reserved liquid, tomato paste and flour until smooth. Return mixture to slow cooker; cover and cook 15 minutes or until thickened. Serve over egg noodles, if desired.   *Makes 6 servings*

NOTE: Coq au Vin is a classical French dish that is made with bone-in chicken, salt pork or bacon, brandy, red wine and herbs. The dish originated when farmers needed a way to cook old chickens that could no longer breed. A slow, moist cooking method was needed to tenderize the tough old birds.

Coq au Vin

144

MAIN DISHES

"FRIED" CHICKEN

1 (2-to 3-pound) whole chicken,
   cut into serving pieces
1 cup all-purpose flour
1 teaspoon salt
1 teaspoon paprika
1 teaspoon dried sage leaves or
   dried oregano leaves
$1/4$ teaspoon garlic powder
$1/8$ teaspoon black pepper
   Butter or vegetable oil

Rinse chicken pieces and pat dry. Combine flour with remaining ingredients except butter. Toss chicken pieces with flour mixture to coat. In skillet, heat butter to $1/4$-inch depth and cook chicken over medium-high heat until golden brown. Place browned chicken in CROCK-POT® Slow Cooker, adding wings first; add no liquid. Cover and cook on Low 8 to 10 hours or on High 4 to 5 hours.   *Makes 4 servings*

CHICKEN 'N' OLIVES

1 (3-pound) whole chicken, cut
   into serving pieces
   Salt and black pepper
1 can (8 ounces) tomato sauce
1 large onion, chopped
$3/4$ cup beer
$1/2$ cup pimiento-stuffed olives
1 clove garlic, minced
2 bay leaves
   Hot cooked rice

Rinse chicken pieces and pat dry. Lightly season with salt and pepper. Combine all ingredients except chicken and rice in CROCK-POT® Slow Cooker; stir well. Add chicken pieces, coating well; be sure all chicken is moistened. Cover and cook on Low 7 to 9 hours. Serve over rice.   *Makes 4 to 6 servings*

MAIN DISHES

CHICKEN DELICIOUS

4 to 6 whole boneless chicken
   breasts, cut into halves
Lemon juice
Salt and pepper
Celery salt
Paprika
1 can (10¾ ounces) condensed
   cream of mushroom soup
1 can (10¾ ounces) condensed
   cream of celery soup
⅓ cup dry sherry or white wine
Grated Parmesan cheese
Hot cooked rice

Rinse chicken breasts and pat dry. Season with lemon juice, salt, pepper, celery salt and paprika. Place in CROCK-POT® Slow Cooker. In medium bowl or pan, mix mushroom and celery soups with sherry. Pour over chicken breasts. Sprinkle with Parmesan cheese. Cover and cook on Low 8 to 10 hours or on High 4 to 5 hours.

Serve chicken and sauce over hot cooked rice.

Makes 8 to 12 servings

MAIN DISHES

CHICKEN LICKIN'

6 to 8 chicken legs, thighs or
    breasts
3 tablespoons butter or margarine
1 can (16 ounces) whole tomatoes
1 large onion, chopped
1 can (4 ounces) sliced
    mushrooms, drained
1 clove garlic, minced
2 teaspoons paprika
1 teaspoon salt
½ teaspoon ground ginger
½ teaspoon chili powder
½ cup heavy cream (optional)
    Hot cooked spaghetti

Rinse chicken parts and pat dry. In skillet, melt butter and brown chicken quickly on both sides. Place chicken in CROCK-POT® Slow Cooker. Stir together remaining ingredients except cream and spaghetti; pour over chicken. Cover and cook on Low 8 to 10 hours or on High 4 to 5 hours. Just before serving, stir in heavy cream. Serve over hot spaghetti. *Makes 6 to 8 servings*

CHICKEN PARMESAN

2 cans (10¾ ounces each) cream
    of mushroom soup, undiluted
1½ cups milk
1 cup white cooking wine
1 cup uncooked converted white
    rice
1 package onion soup mix
6 boneless skinless chicken
    breasts
6 tablespoons margarine or butter
  Salt to taste
  Black pepper to taste
  Grated Parmesan cheese

Mix cream of mushroom soup, milk, wine, rice and onion soup mix in small mixing bowl. Spray CROCK-POT® Slow Cooker with cooking spray. Lay chicken breasts in CROCK-POT® Slow Cooker. Place 1 tablespoon margarine on each chicken breast. Pour soup mixture over chicken breasts. Add salt and pepper to taste. Sprinkle with grated Parmesan cheese. Cook on Low 8 to 10 hours or on High 4 to 6 hours. *Makes 6 servings*

CHICKEN FAJITAS WITH COWPOKE BARBECUE SAUCE

SAUCE

- 1 can (8 ounces) tomato sauce
- 1/3 cup chopped green onions
- 1/4 cup ketchup
- 2 tablespoons water
- 2 tablespoons orange juice
- 1 tablespoon cider vinegar
- 1 tablespoon chili sauce
- 2 cloves garlic, finely chopped
- 1/2 teaspoon vegetable oil
  Dash Worcestershire sauce

FAJITAS

- Nonstick cooking spray
- 10 ounces boneless skinless chicken breasts, cut lengthwise into 1×1/2-inch pieces
- 2 green or red bell peppers, thinly sliced
- 1 cup sliced onion
- 2 cups tomato wedges
- 4 (6-inch) warm flour tortillas

Combine all Cowpoke Barbecue Sauce ingredients in slow cooker. Cover and cook on High 1½ hours.

Spray large nonstick skillet with nonstick cooking spray. Add chicken and cook over medium heat until browned. Reduce slow cooker heat to Low. Add cooked chicken, bell peppers and onion to slow cooker. Stir until well coated. Cover and cook 3 to 4 hours or until chicken is no longer pink and vegetables are tender.

Add tomatoes; cover and cook 30 to 45 minutes or until heated through. Serve with warm tortillas. *Makes 4 servings*

CHICKEN PIE

3 cups diced cooked chicken or
    turkey
3 cups cubed peeled potatoes
2 cans (14½ ounces each) chicken
    broth
1 package (16 ounces) frozen
    mixed vegetables
1 medium onion, chopped
1 stalk celery, thinly sliced
1½ teaspoons black pepper, divided
1 teaspoon salt, divided
1 bay leaf
1 cup milk
1 cup all-purpose flour
½ teaspoon poultry seasoning
1 (9-inch) refrigerated pie crust

In CROCK-POT® Slow Cooker, combine chicken, potatoes, chicken broth, mixed vegetables, onion, celery, ½ teaspoon black pepper, ½ teaspoon salt and bay leaf. Cover; cook on Low 8 to 10 hours or on High 4 to 6 hours. Remove bay leaf.

Preheat oven to 400°F. In small bowl, mix milk and flour. Gradually stir flour mixture into CROCK-POT® Slow Cooker. Stir in remaining 1 teaspoon pepper, poultry seasoning and remaining ½ teaspoon salt. If using a removable CROCK-POT® Slow Cooker, carefully place 9-inch pie crust over vegetable-meat mixture. Place removable crock inside preheated oven; *do not cover*. Bake 15 minutes or until crust is browned. For a non-removable CROCK-POT® Slow Cooker, spoon vegetable-meat mixture into 13×9-inch casserole dish. Roll out pie crust and carefully place on top of vegetable-meat mixture. Bake in oven for 15 minutes or until pie crust is brown. Serve immediately.

Makes 8 servings

FORTY–CLOVE CHICKEN

 1 (3-pound) whole chicken, cut
    into serving pieces
    Salt and black pepper
 1 to 2 tablespoons olive oil
 ¼ cup dry white wine
 ⅛ cup dry vermouth
 2 tablespoons chopped fresh
    parsley *or* 2 teaspoons dried
    parsley leaves
 2 teaspoons dried basil leaves
 1 teaspoon dried oregano leaves
    Dash red pepper flakes
40 cloves garlic (about 2 heads*),
    peeled
 4 ribs celery, sliced
    Juice and peel of 1 lemon
    Fresh herbs (optional)

The whole garlic bulb is called a head.

Remove skin from chicken, if desired. Sprinkle with salt and pepper. Heat oil in large skillet over medium heat. Add chicken; cook 10 minutes or until browned on all sides. Remove to platter.

Combine wine, vermouth, parsley, basil, oregano and red pepper flakes in large bowl. Add garlic and celery; coat well. Transfer garlic and celery to slow cooker with slotted spoon. Add chicken to remaining herb mixture; coat well. Place chicken on top of celery in slow cooker. Sprinkle lemon juice and peel in slow cooker; add remaining herb mixture. Cover and cook on Low 6 hours or until chicken is no longer pink in center. Garnish with fresh herbs, if desired. *Makes 4 to 6 servings*

Forty-Clove Chicken

CHICKEN 'N' RICE IN A BAG

1 (3-pound) whole chicken, cut into serving pieces
1 can (10¾ ounces) condensed cream of chicken soup
1 cup uncooked long-grain converted rice
⅔ cup water
1 envelope (1½ ounces) dry onion soup mix

Rinse chicken pieces and pat dry; set aside. Combine cream of chicken soup, rice and water in CROCK-POT® Slow Cooker; stir well to mix in soup. Place chicken pieces in see-through roasting bag; add onion soup mix. Shake bag to coat chicken pieces thoroughly. Puncture 4 to 6 holes in bottom of bag. Fold top of bag over chicken and place in CROCK-POT® Slow Cooker on top of rice. Cover and cook on Low 8 to 10 hours or on High 4 to 5 hours. Remove chicken pieces to warm platter. Serve with rice.

Makes 4 servings

LEMONY ROASTED CHICKEN

1 (3- to 4-pound) whole chicken
½ cup chopped onion
2 tablespoons butter
Juice of 1 lemon
1 tablespoon fresh parsley
2 teaspoons grated lemon peel
¼ teaspoon salt
¼ teaspoon dried thyme leaves

Rinse chicken and pat dry with paper towels. Remove and discard any excess fat. Place onion in chicken cavity and rub skin with butter. Place chicken in slow cooker. Squeeze lemon juice over chicken. Sprinkle with grated lemon peel, salt and thyme. Cover and cook on Low 6 to 8 hours.

Makes 6 servings

INTERNATIONAL CHICKEN

1 (3-pound) whole chicken, cut into serving pieces
¼ cup plus 3 tablespoons all-purpose flour, divided
2 teaspoons salt
2 teaspoons curry powder
⅛ teaspoon black pepper
1 large onion, chopped
1 large green bell pepper, seeded and sliced into rings
½ cup raisins
1 cloves garlic, minced
1 can (16 ounces) whole tomatoes, mashed
3 tablespoons water

Rinse chicken and pat dry. Combine ¼ cup flour, salt, curry powder and pepper. Dust chicken well with flour mixture. Place coated chicken in CROCK-POT® Slow Cooker and mix in chopped vegetables, raisins and garlic. Pour tomatoes over all. Cover and cook on Low 8 to 10 hours or on High 3 to 4 hours.

Remove chicken pieces to warm platter. Thicken sauce before serving by stirring a smooth paste of remaining 3 tablespoons flour and water into sauce in CROCK-POT® Slow Cooker. Cover and cook on High until sauce is thickened. Spoon sauce over top.

Makes 4 servings

HOT CHICKEN SALAD

2½ cups diced cooked chicken
2 cups diagonally sliced celery
1 cup toasted almonds
1 cup mayonnaise
1 cup cubed processed cheese, divided
1 cup crushed potato chips, divided
½ cup grated Parmesan cheese, divided
½ cup diced green bell pepper
3 tablespoons grated onion
3 tablespoons lemon juice
Toasted English muffins

Combine all ingredients in CROCK-POT® Slow Cooker except half of processed cheese, half of potato chips, half of Parmesan cheese and English muffins. Cover and cook on Low 4 to 6 hours.

Just before serving, sprinkle with remaining processed cheese, potato chips and Parmesan cheese. Serve on toasted English muffins. *Makes 6 to 8 servings*

HOT TURKEY SALAD: Substitute diced cooked turkey for chicken.

MAIN DISHES

SOUPER CHICKEN

2 pounds chicken parts
1 can (10¾ ounces) condensed
    cream of celery soup
¼ cup all-purpose flour
2 medium zucchini, cut
    lengthwise and sliced
    diagonally into ½-inch pieces
1 cup drained canned tomato
    wedges
1 clove garlic, minced
1 teaspoon paprika
½ teaspoon dried basil leaves

Rinse chicken parts and pat dry. Mix soup with flour. Combine all ingredients in CROCK-POT® Slow Cooker; stir thoroughly to coat chicken. Cover and cook on Low 8 to 10 hours or on High 4 to 5 hours.

Makes 4 servings

TERIYAKI CHICKEN

2 pounds boneless skinless chicken breasts
1 package (16 ounces) frozen broccoli, carrots and water chestnuts
2 tablespoons quick-cooking tapioca
1 cup chicken broth
4 tablespoons brown sugar
4 tablespoons teriyaki sauce
2 tablespoons dry mustard
1½ teaspoons grated orange peel
1 teaspoon ground ginger
Hot cooked rice

Rinse chicken and pat dry. Cut chicken into 1-inch pieces. Place frozen vegetables in CROCK-POT® Slow Cooker. Sprinkle with tapioca. Place chicken pieces on top of vegetables. In small bowl, mix chicken broth, brown sugar, teriyaki sauce, mustard, orange peel and ginger. Pour sauce over chicken pieces. Cover; cook on Low 4 to 6 hours or on High 2 to 3 hours. Serve over hot cooked rice.

Makes 4 servings

SPICY TURKEY MEATBALLS

1 pound ground turkey
1 cup plain bread crumbs
¼ cup minced onion
1 egg white
2 tablespoons chopped parsley
1 tablespoon rubbed sage
1 clove garlic, minced *or*
    ⅛ teaspoon garlic powder
1 teaspoon grated orange peel
¼ teaspoon salt
¼ teaspoon cayenne pepper
    Black pepper to taste
1 tablespoon olive oil or vegetable
    oil
1 jar (16 ounces) spaghetti sauce

Combine ground turkey, bread crumbs, onion, egg white, parsley, sage, garlic, orange peel, salt, cayenne and black pepper. Form into 1-inch balls and brown in skillet with oil. Drain meatballs and place in CROCK-POT® Slow Cooker. Cook on High 1 hour; stir in spaghetti sauce. Cook on Low 4 to 6 hours or on High 2 to 3 hours. Serve over cooked spaghetti or fettuccine.

Makes 6 to 8 servings

THAI TURKEY & NOODLES

  1 package (about 1½ pounds) turkey tenderloins, cut into ¾-inch pieces
  1 red bell pepper, cut into short, thin strips
1¼ cups reduced-sodium chicken broth, divided
  ¼ cup reduced-sodium soy sauce
  3 cloves garlic, minced
  ¾ teaspoon red pepper flakes
  ¼ teaspoon salt
  2 tablespoons cornstarch
  3 green onions, cut into ½-inch pieces
  ⅓ cup creamy or chunky peanut butter (not natural-style)
 12 ounces hot cooked vermicelli pasta
  ¾ cup peanuts or cashews, chopped
  ¾ cup cilantro, chopped

Place turkey, bell pepper, 1 cup broth, soy sauce, garlic, red pepper flakes and salt in slow cooker. Cover and cook on Low 3 hours.

Mix cornstarch with remaining ¼ cup broth in small bowl until smooth. Turn slow cooker to High. Stir in green onions, peanut butter and cornstarch mixture. Cover and cook 30 minutes or until sauce is thickened and turkey is no longer pink in center. Stir well. Serve over vermicelli. Sprinkle with peanuts and cilantro.

Makes 6 servings

TIP: If you don't have vermicelli on hand, try substituting ramen noodles. Discard the flavor packet from ramen soup mix and drop the noodles into boiling water. Cook the noodles 2 to 3 minutes or until just tender. Drain and serve hot.

Thai Turkey & Noodles

GROUND TURKEY TACOS

1 pound ground turkey
1 medium onion, chopped
1 can (6 ounces) tomato paste
1 can (4 ounces) sliced
    mushrooms, drained
½ cup white cooking wine
1 tablespoon chopped parsley
1 clove garlic, minced *or*
    ⅛ teaspoon garlic powder
½ teaspoon salt
1 teaspoon pickling spices
4 whole peppercorns
8 taco shells

Brown turkey and onion in skillet over medium heat. In CROCK-POT® Slow Cooker, combine turkey, onion, tomato paste, mushrooms, wine, parsley, garlic and salt. Tie pickling spices and peppercorns in cheesecloth bag or tea ball. Add to CROCK-POT® Slow Cooker; cover and cook on Low 4 to 5 hours. Remove spice bag. Prepare Cream Sauce. Spoon ¼ cup turkey mixture into each taco shell. Top with Cream Sauce.   *Makes about 8 tacos*

CREAM SAUCE MADE WITH YOGURT

1 tablespoon margarine or butter
1 tablespoon all-purpose flour
¼ teaspoon salt
⅓ cup milk
1 egg, slightly beaten
½ cup plain yogurt
    Dash ground nutmeg

In small saucepan, melt margarine; stir in flour and salt. Gradually add milk, stirring continuously. Cook over low heat until thickened. Remove from heat. In small bowl, combine egg, yogurt and nutmeg. Stir into hot mixture. Return to heat and cook over low heat 1 minute, stirring continuously.

Makes about ⅔ cup

TURKEY MEATBALLS WITH GRAVY

2 eggs, beaten
¾ cup seasoned bread crumbs
½ cup chopped onion
½ cup finely chopped celery
2 tablespoons chopped parsley
½ teaspoon poultry seasoning
¼ teaspoon black pepper
⅛ teaspoon garlic powder
2 pounds ground turkey
1 to 2 teaspoons vegetable oil
1 can (10¾ ounces) cream of mushroom soup, undiluted
1 cup water
1 envelope ($^{15}/_{16}$ ounce) turkey gravy mix
½ teaspoon shredded lemon peel
¼ teaspoon dried thyme leaves
1 bay leaf
   Hot cooked mashed potatoes or buttered noodles

In large bowl, combine eggs, bread crumbs, onion, celery, parsley, poultry seasoning, pepper and garlic powder. Add ground turkey and mix well. Shape into 1-inch balls.

In large skillet, brown meatballs in oil. Drain meatballs. Transfer to CROCK-POT® Slow Cooker. In bowl, combine soup, water, gravy mix, lemon peel, thyme and bay leaf. Pour over meatballs. Cover and cook on Low 6 to 8 hours or on High 3 to 4 hours. Discard bay leaf. Serve with mashed potatoes or buttered noodles.

Makes 8 servings

TURKEY ENCHILADAS

8 (6-inch) corn tortillas
1 can (10 ounces) enchilada sauce
1 can (15½ ounces) dark red
    kidney beans
1 cup shredded cooked turkey
1 cup shredded taco-flavored
    cheese

Make foil handles using method on page 7; place in CROCK-POT® Slow Cooker. Place 1 corn tortilla in bottom of CROCK-POT® Slow Cooker. Spoon small amount of enchilada sauce, beans, turkey and cheese over tortilla. Continue layering process until tortillas are gone. Make sure that last layer is cheese layer. Cook on Low 6 to 8 hours or on High 3 to 4 hours. Pull out by foil handles and slice into pie shaped wedges for serving.

Makes 4 servings

TURKEY OLÉ

4 cups cooked turkey, shredded
2 cans (6 ounces each) tomato
    paste
½ cup water
1 package (1⅝ ounces) enchilada
    sauce mix
1 cup shredded Monterey Jack
    cheese
  Corn chips
  Garnish: sour cream, sliced
    green onions, sliced black
    olives

Stir turkey, tomato paste, water and sauce mix into CROCK-POT® Slow Cooker. Cover; cook on Low 7 to 8 hours or on High 3 to 4 hours. If on Low, turn to High and add cheese. Allow cheese to melt. Serve with corn chips. Garnish with sour cream, green onions and olives. *Makes 4 to 6 servings*

VARIATION: Serve over cooked rice or noodles rather than with corn chips. Delicious also as filling for tacos or tostadas.

Turkey Enchiladas

CHILI TURKEY LOAF

2 pounds ground turkey
1 cup chopped onion
²/₃ cup Italian-style seasoned dry
    bread crumbs
½ cup chopped green bell pepper
½ cup chili sauce
2 eggs, lightly beaten
2 tablespoons horseradish
    mustard
4 cloves garlic, minced
1 teaspoon salt
½ teaspoon Italian seasoning
¼ teaspoon black pepper
    Prepared salsa (optional)

Make foil handles for loaf using technique described on page 7. Mix all ingredients except salsa in large bowl. Shape into round loaf and place on top of foil strips. Transfer to bottom of slow cooker using foil handles. Cover and cook on Low 4½ to 5 hours or until juices run clear and internal temperature is 170°F. Remove loaf from slow cooker using foil handles. Place on serving plate. Let stand 5 minutes before serving. Cut into wedges and top with salsa, if desired. Serve with steamed carrots, if desired.

Makes 8 servings

Chili Turkey Loaf

SWEET AND SOUR TURKEY

3 cups uncooked converted white rice

2 bottles (11½ ounces each) sweet and sour sauce, divided

1 package (16 ounces) frozen broccoli, cauliflower, pea pods and yellow peppers, thawed and drained

2 to 3 cups water

1 cup cubed cooked turkey

1 can (11 ounces) Mandarin orange slices

1 can (8 ounces) pineapple chunks

In CROCK-POT® Slow Cooker, combine rice, 1 bottle sweet and sour sauce, vegetables, water and turkey. Cook on Low 6 to 8 hours or High 3 to 4 hours. During last 30 minutes of cooking, stir in canned fruit and remaining bottle of sweet and sour sauce.

Makes 4 servings

TURKEY AND CORN CASSEROLE

1 tablespoon margarine or butter
1 onion, chopped
1 can (16 ounces) cream-style corn
4 large eggs
½ cup evaporated milk
⅓ cup all-purpose flour
  Salt to taste
  Black pepper to taste
2 cups chopped cooked turkey
1 cup (4 ounces) shredded Cheddar cheese (sharp or mild)

In large skillet, melt margarine over medium heat. Add onion; cook, stirring often, until softened (about 5 minutes). Transfer mixture to medium bowl. Whisk corn, eggs, evaporated milk, flour, salt and pepper into onion mixture. Stir in turkey. Transfer to lightly greased CROCK-POT® Slow Cooker.

Cover and cook on High 2½ to 3 hours or until knife inserted comes out clean.

Sprinkle top of casserole with cheese; cover and cook until cheese is melted, about 15 minutes. Serve immediately.

Makes 4 servings

TURKEY TACOS

1 pound ground turkey
1 medium onion, chopped
1 can (6 ounces) tomato paste
½ cup chunky salsa
1 tablespoon chopped cilantro
½ plus ¼ teaspoon salt, divided
8 taco shells
1 tablespoon butter
1 tablespoon all-purpose flour
⅓ cup milk
½ cup sour cream
  Ground red pepper to taste

Brown turkey and onion in large skillet over medium heat. Combine turkey mixture, tomato paste, salsa, cilantro and ½ teaspoon salt in slow cooker. Cover and cook on Low 4 to 5 hours. Spoon ¼ cup turkey mixture into each taco shell; keep warm.

Melt butter in small saucepan over low heat. Stir in flour and remaining ¼ teaspoon salt. Carefully stir in milk. Cook over low heat until thickened. Remove from heat. Combine sour cream and red pepper in small bowl. Stir into hot milk mixture. Return to heat; cook over low heat 1 minute, stirring constantly. Top each taco with sour cream mixture. *Makes 8 tacos*

MAIN DISHES

SOUPER RICE AND TURKEY

3 cups water
2 cans (10¾ ounces each)
    condensed cream of
    mushroom soup
3 cups uncooked converted white
    rice
2 cups frozen peas and carrots or
    frozen oriental vegetable mix
1 cup cubed cooked turkey
1 cup thinly sliced celery
1 tablespoon minced onion
1 teaspoon poultry seasoning

Pour water and soup into CROCK-POT® Slow Cooker; mix. Add remaining ingredients and stir. Cook on Low 6 to 8 hours or on High 3 to 4 hours. Add soy sauce, if desired.   *Makes 4 servings*

SPICED TURKEY LOAF

2 to 2½ pounds ground turkey
1 medium onion, chopped
1 cup bread crumbs
⅓ cup milk
2 eggs, lightly beaten
¼ cup chopped parsley
¼ cup bottled chili sauce
2 tablespoons horseradish
2 cloves garlic, minced
1 teaspoon salt

Mix all ingredients together in large bowl. Form into loaf and lay atop meat rack or use foil handles (see page 7). Cook turkey loaf on Low 8 to 10 hours or on High 5 to 6 hours. To ensure doneness, insert meat thermometer in loaf. Thermometer should read 180°F to indicate doneness. Serve with sour cream, if desired.   *Makes 8 servings*

BARBECUED BEEF

    3 pounds boneless chuck roast
1½ cups ketchup
    ¼ cup packed brown sugar
    ¼ cup red wine vinegar
    2 tablespoons Dijon mustard
    2 tablespoons Worcestershire
        sauce
    1 teaspoon liquid smoke flavoring
    ½ teaspoon salt
    ¼ teaspoon black pepper
    ¼ teaspoon garlic powder

Place chuck roast in CROCK-POT® Slow Cooker. Combine remaining ingredients in mixing bowl. Pour barbecue sauce mixture over chuck roast. Cover and cook on Low 8 to 10 hours or on High 4 to 5 hours. Remove chuck roast from CROCK-POT® Slow Cooker; shred meat with fork. Place shredded meat back in CROCK-POT® Slow Cooker. Stir meat to evenly coat with sauce. Spoon meat onto sandwich buns and top with additional barbecue sauce, if desired.   *Makes 12 servings*

Barbecued Beef

BEEF FAJITAS

1½ pounds beef flank steak
1 cup chopped onion
1 green bell pepper, cut into
    ½-inch pieces
1 jalapeño pepper,* chopped
1 tablespoon cilantro
2 cloves garlic, minced *or*
    ¼ teaspoon garlic powder
1 teaspoon chili powder
1 teaspoon ground cumin
1 teaspoon ground coriander
½ teaspoon salt
1 can (8 ounces) chopped
    tomatoes
12 (8-inch) flour tortillas
    Toppings: sour cream,
    guacamole, shredded
    Cheddar cheese, salsa

*If using fresh jalapeño peppers, be very careful when handling. Wear rubber gloves if possible as jalapeño peppers contain a volatile oil that will burn if left in direct contact with the skin. Wash hands immediately after handling.

Cut flank steak into 6 portions. In any size CROCK-POT® Slow Cooker, combine steak, onion, bell pepper, jalapeño pepper, cilantro, garlic, chili powder, cumin, coriander and salt. Add tomatoes. Cover and cook on Low 8 to 10 hours or on High 4 to 5 hours.

Remove meat from CROCK-POT® Slow Cooker and shred with fork. Return meat to CROCK-POT® Slow Cooker and stir. To serve fajitas, spread meat mixture into flour tortillas and top with toppings, if desired. Roll up tortillas.   *Makes 12 servings*

Beef Fajita

AMERICA'S FAVORITE POT ROAST

3½ to 4 pounds beef arm or
    boneless pot roast
¼ cup plus 3 tablespoons
    all-purpose flour, divided
2 teaspoons salt
⅛ teaspoon black pepper
3 potatoes, peeled and quartered
3 carrots, peeled, sliced
    lengthwise and cut into
    2-inch pieces
2 small onions, sliced
1 stalk celery, cut into 2-inch
    pieces
1 jar (2 ounces) mushrooms,
    drained *or* ¼ cup mushroom
    gravy
¼ cup water

Trim all excess fat from roast; brown and drain if using chuck or another highly marbled cut. Combine ¼ cup flour, salt and pepper in small bowl. Coat meat with flour mixture. Place all vegetables except mushrooms in CROCK-POT® Slow Cooker and top with roast (cut roast in half, if necessary, to fit easily). Spread mushrooms evenly over top of roast. Cover and cook on Low 10 to 12 hours.

If desired, turn to High during last hour to soften vegetables and make gravy. To thicken gravy, make smooth paste with remaining 3 tablespoons flour and water; stir into CROCK-POT® Slow Cooker. Season to taste before serving.

Makes 4 to 6 servings

VEGETABLE BEEF

1 (3- to 4-pound) beef round or
    chuck steak, 1½ inches thick,
    cut into 1½-inch cubes
⅓ cup plus ¼ cup all-purpose
    flour, divided
1 teaspoon salt
½ teaspoon cracked black pepper
2 to 3 carrots, peeled, split
    lengthwise and cut in half
2 large stalks celery, cut into
    1-inch pieces
6 small white onions
6 to 8 small new potatoes, peeled
1 package (10 ounces) frozen
    peas, corn, green beans or
    lima beans, partially thawed
1 can (4 ounces) sliced
    mushrooms, drained
1 can (10½ ounces) condensed
    beef broth
½ cup dry red wine or water
2 teaspoons brown sugar
2 teaspoons Kitchen Bouquet
1 can (14½ ounces) tomato
    wedges or slices, drained
    (optional)
¼ cup water

If beef is extra lean, thoroughly wipe cubed beef on absorbent towels to dry. If meat contains fat, quickly brown in large skillet to sear and remove fat; drain well.

Place beef cubes in CROCK-POT® Slow Cooker. Combine ⅓ cup flour, salt and pepper; toss with beef to coat thoroughly. Add all vegetables except tomato wedges to CROCK-POT® Slow Cooker and mix well. Combine beef broth, wine, sugar and Kitchen Bouquet. Pour over meat and vegetables; stir carefully. Add drained tomatoes and stir well. Cover and cook on Low 10 to 14 hours or on High 4 to 5½ hours.

One hour before serving, turn to High. Make a smooth paste with remaining ¼ cup flour and water; stir into CROCK-POT® Slow Cooker. Cover and cook until thickened.

Makes 8 to 10 servings

NOTE: For better color, add half of the frozen vegetables at beginning; add remaining half during last hour.

BEEF AND PARSNIP STROGANOFF

1 cube beef bouillon

¾ cup boiling water

¾ pound well-trimmed boneless top round beef steak, 1 inch thick

Nonstick olive oil cooking spray

2 cups cubed peeled parsnips or potatoes*

1 medium onion, halved and thinly sliced

¾ pound mushrooms, sliced

2 teaspoons minced garlic

¼ teaspoon black pepper

¼ cup water

1 tablespoon plus 1½ teaspoons all-purpose flour

3 tablespoons reduced-fat sour cream

1½ teaspoons Dijon mustard

¼ teaspoon cornstarch

1 tablespoon chopped parsley

4 ounces cholesterol-free wide noodles, cooked without salt, drained and kept hot

*If using potatoes, cut into 1-inch chunks and do not sauté.

1. Dissolve bouillon cube in ¾ cup boiling water; cool. Meanwhile, cut steak into 2×½-inch strips. Spray large nonstick skillet with cooking spray; heat over high heat. Cook and stir beef about 4 minutes or until meat begins to brown and is barely pink. Transfer beef and juices to slow cooker.

2. Spray same skillet with cooking spray; heat over high heat. Add parsnips and onion; cook and stir until browned, about 4 minutes. Add mushrooms, garlic and pepper; cook and stir until mushrooms are tender, about 5 minutes. Transfer mushroom mixture to slow cooker; mix with beef.

3. Blend ¼ cup water and flour in small bowl until smooth. Stir flour mixture into cooled bouillon. Add to slow cooker. Cook, covered, on Low 4½ to 5 hours or until beef and parsnips are tender.

4. Turn off slow cooker. Remove beef and vegetables with slotted spoon to large bowl; reserve cooking liquid from beef. Blend sour cream, mustard and cornstarch in medium bowl. Gradually add reserved liquid to sour cream mixture; stir well to blend. Stir sour cream mixture into beef mixture. Sprinkle with parsley; serve over noodles. Garnish, if desired. *Makes 4 servings*

MAIN DISHES

BEEF DIABLO

3 to 4 pounds beef arm or
   boneless pot roast
2 to 3 potatoes, peeled and sliced
1 onion, sliced
2 tablespoons all-purpose flour
1 tablespoon prepared mustard
1 tablespoon chili sauce
1 tablespoon Worcestershire
   sauce
1 teaspoon vinegar
1 teaspoon sugar

Trim all excess fat from roast. Place potatoes and onion in bottom of CROCK-POT® Slow Cooker.

Make a smooth paste with flour, mustard, chili sauce, Worcestershire sauce, vinegar and sugar. Spread over top of roast (cut roast in half, if necessary, to fit easily). Place roast in CROCK-POT® Slow Cooker on top of potatoes and onions. Cover and cook on Low 10 to 12 hours or on High 5 to 6 hours.

Makes 4 to 6 servings

BEEF HASH

2 to 3 cups cut-up cooked beef
2 packages (10 ounces each)
   frozen hash brown potatoes,
   thawed
1 cup gravy or beef broth
1 onion, finely chopped
¼ cup butter or margarine, melted
   Salt and black pepper

Place all ingredients in CROCK-POT® Slow Cooker. Cover and cook on Low 6 to 8 hours or on High 2 to 3 hours.

Makes 4 servings

NOTE: Double recipe for 5-quart CROCK-POT® Slow Cooker

FAVORITE BEEF STEW

3 carrots, cut lengthwise into
   halves, then cut into 1-inch
   pieces
3 ribs celery, cut into 1-inch
   pieces
2 large potatoes, peeled and cut
   into ½-inch pieces
1½ cups chopped onions
3 cloves garlic, chopped
1 bay leaf
1½ tablespoons Worcestershire
   sauce
¾ teaspoon dried thyme leaves
¾ teaspoon dried basil leaves
½ teaspoon black pepper
2 pounds lean beef stew meat,
   cut into 1-inch pieces
1 can (14½ ounces) diced
   tomatoes, undrained
1 can (about 14 ounces)
   reduced-sodium beef broth
¼ cup all-purpose flour
½ cup cold water

Layer ingredients in slow cooker in the following order: carrots, celery, potatoes, onions, garlic, bay leaf, Worcestershire sauce, thyme, basil, pepper, beef, tomatoes with juice and broth. Cover and cook on Low 8 to 9 hours.

Remove beef and vegetables to large serving bowl; cover and keep warm. Remove and discard bay leaf. Turn slow cooker to High; cover. Mix flour and water in small bowl until smooth. Add ½ cup cooking liquid; mix well. Stir flour mixture into slow cooker. Cover and cook 15 minutes or until thickened. Pour sauce over meat and vegetables. Serve immediately.

Makes 6 to 8 servings

Favorite Beef Stew

BAVARIAN POT ROAST

3 to 4 pounds beef arm pot roast
1 teaspoon vegetable oil
1 teaspoon salt
½ teaspoon ground ginger
⅛ teaspoon black pepper
3 whole cloves
4 medium apples, cored and
    quartered
1 small onion, sliced
½ cup apple juice or water
3 to 4 tablespoons all-purpose
    flour
3 to 4 tablespoons water

Wipe roast well and trim off excess fat. Lightly rub top of roast with oil. Dust with salt, ginger and pepper. Insert cloves in roast. Place apples and onion in CROCK-POT® Slow Cooker and top with roast (cut roast in half, if necessary, to fit easily). Pour in apple juice. Cover and cook on Low 10 to 12 hours or on High 5 to 6 hours.

Remove roast and apples to warm platter. Turn CROCK-POT® Slow Cooker to High. Make a smooth paste with flour and water; stir into CROCK-POT® Slow Cooker. Cover and cook until thickened. Pour over roast. *Makes 6 to 8 servings*

GLAZED CORNED BEEF

1½ cups water
  1 medium onion, sliced
  3 strips fresh orange peel
  2 whole cloves
  3 to 4 pounds corned beef (round or rump cut)
  Additional whole cloves (optional)
  Glaze (recipe follows)

Combine water, onion, orange peel and cloves in slow cooker. Add corned beef, fat side up, to slow cooker. Cover and cook on Low 7 to 9 hours or until fork tender.

Remove corned beef from slow cooker. Score top of corned beef; insert additional cloves to decorate, if desired.

About 30 minutes before serving, place corned beef in ovenproof pan. Preheat oven to 375°F. Prepare Glaze; spoon over corned beef. Bake 20 to 30 minutes, basting occasionally with Glaze.

Makes 8 to 10 servings

GLAZE

  2 tablespoons frozen orange juice concentrate, thawed
  3 tablespoons honey
  2 teaspoons prepared mustard

Combine orange juice concentrate, honey and mustard in large bowl.

SWISS STEAK

2 pounds beef round steak, about
    1 inch thick
¼ cup all-purpose flour
1 teaspoon salt
1 stalk celery, chopped
2 carrots, peeled and chopped
¼ cup chopped onion
½ teaspoon Worcestershire sauce
1 can (8 ounces) tomato sauce
½ cup grated processed American
    cheese (optional)

Cut steak into 4 serving pieces. Dredge in flour mixed with salt; place in CROCK-POT® Slow Cooker. Add chopped vegetables and Worcestershire sauce. Pour tomato sauce over meat and vegetables. Cover and cook on Low 8 to 10 hours or on High 4 to 5 hours.

Just before serving, sprinkle with grated cheese.

Makes 4 servings

NOTE: Recipe may be doubled for 5-quart CROCK-POT® Slow Cooker. Cook the maximum time.

MARINATED BARBECUE BRISKET

4 to 5 pounds fresh beef brisket
2 teaspoons unseasoned meat
    tenderizer
½ teaspoon celery salt
½ teaspoon seasoned salt
½ teaspoon garlic salt
¼ cup liquid smoke
¼ cup Worcestershire sauce
1½ cups barbecue sauce

Place brisket on large piece of heavy-duty aluminum foil. Sprinkle tenderizer and seasonings on both sides of meat. Pour liquid smoke and Worcestershire sauce over top. Cover and marinate in refrigerator 6 to 10 hours or overnight.

Place foil-wrapped brisket in CROCK-POT® Slow Cooker (cut brisket in half, if necessary, to fit easily). Cover and cook on Low 10 to 12 hours.

Chill brisket, then cut across the grain into thin slices. Before serving, reheat in your favorite barbecue sauce.

Makes 8 to 10 servings

Swiss Steak

FLANK STEAK TERIYAKI

2 pounds beef flank steak
6 slices canned juice-packed
    pineapple (reserve ½ cup
    juice)
2 tablespoons soy sauce
2 tablespoons brown sugar
1 tablespoon dry sherry
1 teaspoon Worcestershire sauce
½ teaspoon ground ginger
2 chicken boullion cubes
1½ cups boiling water
1 cup uncooked long-grain
    converted rice

Roll flank steak; tie and cut into 6 individual steaks. In shallow bowl, stir together pineapple juice, soy sauce, sugar, sherry, Worcestershire sauce and ginger. Marinate steaks about 1 hour in soy mixture at room temperature. Dissolve boullion cubes in boiling water; combine with rice and ½ cup of soy mixture in CROCK-POT® Slow Cooker. Top each steak with pineapple ring, then place in CROCK-POT® Slow Cooker. Cover and cook on Low 8 to 10 hours or on High 3 to 4 hours. *Makes 6 servings*

SAUERBRATEN

    4 pounds beef rump roast
    3 large onions, sliced
    2 stalks celery, sliced
    1 cup dry rosé wine
    ¼ cup cider vinegar
    1 clove garlic
    2 whole allspice berries
    3 to 4 whole cloves
    1 teaspoon salt
    ½ teaspoon black pepper
    3 tablespoons all-purpose flour
    3 tablespoons water
    1 cup crushed gingersnap cookies

Trim roast of all excess fat. In large bowl, combine all ingredients except roast, flour, water and gingersnaps; stir well. Place roast in marinade; refrigerate overnight.

Pour vegetable marinade into CROCK-POT® Slow Cooker. Place marinated roast in CROCK-POT® Slow Cooker with fat side up. Cover and cook on Low for 10 to 12 hours.

Thirty minutes before serving, remove roast and turn to High. Make a smooth paste of flour and water; stir into CROCK-POT® Slow Cooker with gingersnaps. Cook and stir until thickened. Slice roast and return to gravy for serving.

Makes 6 to 8 servings

BEEF TIPS

½ cup plus 3 tablespoons
    all-purpose flour, divided
1 teaspoon salt
⅛ teaspoon black pepper
4 pounds beef or sirloin tips
2 cans (4 ounces each) sliced
    mushrooms, drained *or*
    ½ pound mushrooms, sliced
½ cup chopped shallots or green
    onions
1 can (10½ ounces) condensed
    beef broth
1 teaspoon tomato paste or
    ketchup
1 teaspoon Worcestershire sauce
¼ cup dry red wine or water
    Hot buttered noodles

Combine ½ cup flour, salt and pepper; toss with beef tips to coat thoroughly. Place in CROCK-POT® Slow Cooker. Add mushrooms and shallots. Combine beef broth, tomato paste and Worcestershire sauce. Pour over beef and vegetables; stir well. Cover and cook on Low 8 to 12 hours or on High 4 to 6 hours.

One hour before serving, turn to High. Make a smooth paste of red wine and remaining 3 tablespoons flour; stir into CROCK-POT® Slow Cooker, mixing well. Cover and cook until thickened. Serve over hot buttered noodles. *Makes 8 to 10 servings*

DRIED BEEF 'N' NOODLES

- 3 to 4 ounces dried beef
- 1 package (8 ounces) noodles
- 2 teaspoons vegetable oil
- ¼ cup butter or margarine
- ¼ cup all-purpose flour
- 2 cups evaporated milk
- 1 package (10 ounces) frozen peas or frozen mixed vegetables, partially thawed
- 1 package (8 ounces) sharp processed cheese, grated

Snip dried beef into small pieces; set aside. Cook noodles according to package directions until barely tender. In large bowl, toss noodles with oil; set aside. In saucepan, melt butter over medium heat. Blend in flour until smooth. Gradually stir in evaporated milk. Cook until smooth and thick.

Pour white sauce over noodles; toss to mix. Fold in snipped beef, vegetables and most of grated cheese, reserving a small amount to sprinkle over top; stir well. Pour mixture into well-greased CROCK-POT® Slow Cooker. Sprinkle lightly with reserved cheese. Cover and cook on Low 6 to 10 hours.

Makes 4 to 6 servings

GOOD 'N' EASY STEW

- 3 pounds lean stewing beef, cut into 1½-inch cubes
- 1 can (10½ ounces) condensed cream of mushroom soup or cream of celery soup
- 1 can (4 ounces) sliced mushrooms, drained (optional)
- ½ cup sauterne wine or beef broth
- 1 envelope (1½ ounces) dry onion soup mix

Combine all ingredients in CROCK-POT® Slow Cooker. Cover and cook on Low 10 to 12 hours. If desired, thicken gravy with flour.

Makes 8 serving

HEARTY BEEF RAGOÛT

3 pounds boneless beef chuck, cut into 1-inch cubes
½ cup plus 2 tablespoons all-purpose flour, divided
1 teaspoon salt
¼ teaspoon black pepper
1 package (8 ounces) precooked sausage links, cut into 1-inch pieces
2 cups chopped leeks
3 to 4 stalks celery, chopped
3 potatoes, peeled and cubed
1 can (16 ounces) whole tomatoes
1 teaspoon dried oregano leaves
2 cloves garlic, minced
½ cup beef broth
1 teaspoon Kitchen Bouquet
3 tablespoons water

Dry beef cubes well. Combine ½ cup flour with salt and pepper. Toss beef cubes with flour mixture to coat thoroughly; place in CROCK-POT® Slow Cooker. Add remaining ingredients except remaining 2 tablespoons flour and water in order listed; stir well. Cover and cook on Low 8 to 12 hours or on High 4 to 6 hours.

One hour before serving, turn to High. Make smooth paste with 2 tablespoons flour and water; stir into CROCK-POT® Slow Cooker, mixing well. Cover and cook until thickened.

Makes 8 servings

Hearty Beef Ragoût

SAVORY PEPPER STEAK

1½ to 2 pounds beef round steak, about ½-inch thick
¼ cup all-purpose flour
½ teaspoon salt
⅛ teaspoon black pepper
1 medium onion, chopped
1 small clove garlic, minced
2 large green or red bell peppers, seeded and cut into ½-inch strips
1 can (16 ounces) whole tomatoes, undrained
1 tablespoon beef flavor base (paste or granules)
1 tablespoon soy sauce
2 teaspoons Worcestershire sauce
Hot cooked rice

Cut steak into strips. Combine flour, salt and pepper; toss with steak strips to coat thoroughly. Add to CROCK-POT® Slow Cooker with onion, garlic and half of bell pepper strips; stir.

Combine tomatoes with beef base, soy sauce and Worcestershire sauce. Pour into CROCK-POT® Slow Cooker, coating meat well. Cover and cook on Low 8 to 10 hours.

One hour before serving, turn to High and stir in remaining bell pepper strips. If thickened gravy is desired, make a smooth paste of 3 tablespoons flour and 3 tablespoons water; stir into CROCK-POT® Slow Cooker. Cover and cook until thickened. Serve gravy with pepper steak over hot cooked rice.   *Makes 4 servings*

SWEET AND SOUR BEEF OVER RICE

2 pounds boneless chuck
²⁄₃ cup all-purpose flour
3 teaspoons salt, divided
½ teaspoon black pepper
2 tablespoons margarine or butter
1 tablespoon olive oil
1 large onion, chopped
1 cup water
½ cup ketchup
¼ cup packed brown sugar
¼ cup red wine vinegar
1 tablespoon Worcestershire sauce
  Additional black pepper to taste
4 to 6 carrots, diagonally sliced
  Hot cooked rice

Cut beef into 1-inch cubes. Mix together flour, 2 teaspoons salt and ½ teaspoon black pepper; dredge beef cubes in mixture. In large skillet, heat margarine and olive oil; brown beef cubes. Place browned beef in CROCK-POT® Slow Cooker. Add remaining ingredients except carrots. Cover and cook on Low 8 to 9 hours or on High 4 to 5 hours. Add carrots and cook on Low 1½ hours or on High 30 minutes. Serve over rice. *Makes 6 servings*

MAIN DISHES

YANKEE POT ROAST AND VEGETABLES

1 beef chuck pot roast
    (2½ pounds)
3 medium baking potatoes (about
    1 pound), unpeeled and cut
    into quarters
2 large carrots, cut into ¾-inch
    slices
2 ribs celery, cut into ¾-inch slices
1 medium onion, sliced
1 large parsnip, cut into ¾-inch
    slices
2 bay leaves
1 teaspoon dried rosemary
½ teaspoon dried thyme leaves
½ cup reduced-sodium beef broth

Trim excess fat from meat and discard. Cut into serving pieces; sprinkle with salt and pepper. Combine vegetables, bay leaves, rosemary and thyme in slow cooker. Place beef over vegetables in slow cooker. Pour broth over beef. Cover and cook on Low 8½ to 9 hours or until beef is fork-tender. Remove beef to serving platter. Arrange vegetables around beef. Remove and discard bay leaves.

Makes 6 servings

NOTE: To make gravy, ladle juices into 2-cup measure; let stand 5 minutes. Skim off and discard fat. Measure remaining juices and heat to a boil in small saucepan. For each 1 cup juice, mix 2 tablespoons all-purpose flour with ¼ cup cold water until smooth. Stir mixture into boiling juices. Stir constantly 1 minute or until thickened.

Yankee Pot Roast and Vegetables

TEXAS–STYLE BARBECUED BRISKET

1 beef brisket (3 to 4 pounds), trimmed and cut into halves, if necessary, to fit slow cooker

3 tablespoons Worcestershire sauce

1 tablespoon chili powder

1 teaspoon celery salt

1 teaspoon black pepper

1 teaspoon liquid smoke

2 cloves garlic, minced

2 bay leaves

Barbecue Sauce (recipe follows)

Place meat in resealable plastic food storage bag. Combine Worcestershire sauce, chili powder, celery salt, pepper, liquid smoke, garlic and bay leaves in small bowl. Spread mixture on all sides of meat; seal bag. Refrigerate 24 hours.

Place meat and marinade in slow cooker. Cover and cook on Low 7 hours. Meanwhile, prepare Barbecue Sauce.

Remove meat from slow cooker and pour juices into 2-cup measure; let stand 5 minutes. Skim fat from juices. Remove and discard bay leaves. Stir 1 cup of defatted juices into Barbecue Sauce. Discard remaining juices. Return meat and Barbecue Sauce to slow cooker. Cover and cook on Low 1 hour or until meat is fork-tender. Remove meat and slice across grain. Serve with Barbecue Sauce. *Makes 10 to 12 servings*

BARBECUE SAUCE

2 tablespoons vegetable oil

1 medium onion, chopped

2 cloves garlic, minced

1 cup ketchup

$\frac{1}{2}$ cup molasses

$\frac{1}{4}$ cup cider vinegar

2 teaspoons chili powder

$\frac{1}{2}$ teaspoon dry mustard

Heat oil in medium saucepan over medium heat. Add onion and garlic; cook until onion is tender. Add remaining ingredients. Simmer 5 minutes. *Makes 2½ cups sauce*

Texas-Style Barbecued Brisket

ENGLISH BEEF POT PIE

2 pounds beef round steak, cut into 1-inch cubes
3 tablespoons all-purpose flour
1 teaspoon salt
⅛ teaspoon black pepper
1 can (16 ounces) whole tomatoes, undrained
3 medium potatoes, peeled and sliced
2 medium carrots, peeled and sliced
1 large onion, thinly sliced
Biscuit Topping (below)

Place steak cubes in CROCK-POT® Slow Cooker. Combine flour, salt and pepper; toss with steak to coat thoroughly. Stir in remaining ingredients except Biscuit Topping and mix thoroughly. Cover and cook on Low 8 to 10 hours or on High 4 to 5 hours.

One hour before serving, remove meat and vegetables from CROCK-POT® Slow Cooker and pour into shallow 2½-quart baking dish. Preheat oven to 425°F. Cover meat mixture with Biscuit Topping. Bake 20 to 25 minutes. *Makes 4 servings*

BISCUIT TOPPING

2 cups all-purpose flour
1 teaspoon salt
3 teaspoons baking powder
¼ cup shortening
¾ cup milk

Combine flour, salt and baking powder in large bowl. Cut in shortening until mixture resembles coarse cornmeal. Add milk all at one time; stir well. Pat out on floured board; roll out to cover baking dish.

MAIN DISHES

SMOTHERED FLANK STEAK

2½ pounds beef flank or round steak
　　Salt and black pepper
1 tablespoon Worcestershire
　　sauce
1 tablespoon vegetable oil
　　Paprika
2 medium onions, thinly sliced
½ pound mushrooms, sliced *or*
　　2 cans (4 ounces each) sliced
　　mushrooms, drained
　　Chopped parsley

With sharp knife, score meat about ⅛ inch deep in diamond pattern on top side. Season with salt and pepper. Rub in Worcestershire sauce and oil. Sprinkle top with paprika. Place sliced onions and mushrooms in CROCK-POT® Slow Cooker. Roll flank steak, if necessary, to fit easily, and place on top of onions. Cover and cook on Low 8 to 10 hours or on High 4 to 5 hours.

Remove steak to warm carving platter and cut across grain in thin diagonal slices. Serve with onions and mushrooms, pouring unthickened gravy over all. Sprinkle with parsley.

Makes 6 servings

BEEF ROULADES

1½ pounds beef round steak,
　　½ inch thick
4 slices bacon
¾ cup diced celery
¾ cup diced onion
½ cup diced green bell pepper
1 can (10 ounces) beef gravy

Cut steak into four serving pieces. Place bacon slice on each piece of meat. Mix celery, onion and bell pepper in medium bowl; place about ½ cup mixture on each piece of meat. Roll up meat; secure ends with wooden picks.

Wipe beef rolls with paper towels. Place in CROCK-POT® Slow Cooker. Pour gravy evenly over steaks to thoroughly moisten. Cover CROCK-POT® Slow Cooker and cook on Low 8 to 10 hours or on High 4 to 5 hours. Skim off fat before serving.

Makes 4 servings

BEEF STROGANOFF

1½ pounds beef stew meat, cut into
    1-inch cubes
1 tablespoon vegetable oil
1 jar (4 ounces) sliced mushrooms
1 tablespoon dried minced onion
2 cloves garlic, minced *or*
    ¼ teaspoon garlic powder
½ teaspoon dried oregano leaves
¼ teaspoon salt
¼ teaspoon black pepper
⅛ teaspoon dried thyme leaves
1 bay leaf
1½ cups beef broth
⅓ cup dry cooking sherry
1 carton (8 ounces) dairy sour
    cream
½ cup all-purpose flour
¼ cup water
4 cups hot cooked noodles or rice

In large skillet, brown beef in hot oil. Drain off fat.

In CROCK-POT® Slow Cooker, combine beef, mushrooms, onion, garlic, oregano, salt, pepper, thyme and bay leaf. Pour in beef broth and cooking sherry. Cover; cook on Low 8 to 10 hours or on High 4 to 5 hours. Discard bay leaf.

If using Low heat, turn to High heat. Mix together sour cream, flour and water. Stir about 1 cup of hot liquid into sour cream mixture. Return to cooker; stir to combine. Cover and cook on High 30 minutes or until thickened and bubbly. Serve over noodles or rice. *Makes 6 servings*

Beef Stroganoff

BEEF 'N' BEANS

1 pound dried pinto beans
1 to 2 pounds chuck steak, cut
    into 1-inch cubes
¼ pound salt pork or bacon, diced
1 cup water
1 can (6 ounces) tomato paste
1 tablespoon chili powder
2 cloves garlic, minced
1 teaspoon ground cumin
⅛ to ¼ teaspoon crushed red
    pepper
  Salt to taste

Cover beans with 7 cups unsalted water and bring to a boil over high heat. Boil 10 minutes. Reduce heat to low; cover and simmer 1½ hours or until beans are tender. Discard water. In skillet, brown cubed chuck steak and salt pork over medium-heat; drain well. Add to CROCK-POT® Slow Cooker with soaked pinto beans. Add remaining ingredients; stir well. Cover and cook on High 2 hours, then on Low 7 to 12 hours or cook entire time on High 5 to 8 hours. *Makes 8 servings*

FAVORITE BRISKET

4 pounds fresh beef brisket
2 teaspoons dry mustard
2 teaspoons paprika
1 teaspoon salt
½ to 1 teaspoon garlic powder
⅛ teaspoon black pepper

Trim all excess fat from brisket. Combine seasonings until well blended; rub into brisket. Place meat in CROCK-POT® Slow Cooker with fat side up, cutting to fit if necessary. Cover and cook on Low 10 to 12 hours.

Remove brisket from liquid and cut across the grain into thin slices. Serve au jus. *Makes 6 to 8 servings*

POT ROAST OVER NOODLES

2 to 2½ pounds beef chuck roast
1 tablespoon vegetable oil
2 medium carrots, chopped
2 stalks celery, sliced
1 medium onion, sliced
2 cloves garlic, minced
1 can (14½ ounces) Italian-style
    stewed tomatoes, undrained
1 can (6 ounces) Italian-style
    tomato paste
1 tablespoon quick-cooking
    tapioca
1 tablespoon brown sugar
½ teaspoon salt
½ teaspoon black pepper
1 bay leaf
1 package (8 ounces) hot cooked
    wide noodles

In large skillet, brown roast on all sides in hot oil. Transfer to any size CROCK-POT® Slow Cooker. Add vegetables.

In small bowl, combine tomatoes, tomato paste, tapioca, brown sugar, salt, pepper and bay leaf; pour over meat and vegetables. Cover and cook on Low 10 to 12 hours or on High 5 to 6 hours. Discard bay leaf. Cut up meat and serve over hot cooked noodles. *Makes 8 servings*

PORK CHOPS WITH JALAPEÑO–PECAN CORNBREAD STUFFING

**6 boneless loin pork chops,
    1 inch thick (1½ pounds)
¾ cup chopped onion
¾ cup chopped celery
½ cup coarsely chopped pecans
½ medium jalapeño pepper,*
    seeded and chopped
1 teaspoon rubbed sage
½ teaspoon dried rosemary
⅛ teaspoon black pepper
4 cups unseasoned cornbread
    stuffing mix
1¼ cups reduced-sodium chicken
    broth
1 egg, lightly beaten**

*Jalapeño peppers can sting and irritate the skin;
wear rubber gloves when handling peppers and do
not touch eyes.*

Trim excess fat from pork and discard. Spray large skillet with nonstick cooking spray; heat over medium heat. Add pork; cook 10 minutes or until browned on all sides. Remove; set aside. Add onion, celery, pecans, jalapeño pepper, sage, rosemary and black pepper to skillet. Cook 5 minutes or until tender; set aside.

Combine cornbread stuffing mix, vegetable mixture and broth in medium bowl. Stir in egg. Spoon stuffing mixture into slow cooker. Arrange pork on top. Cover and cook on Low about 5 hours or until pork is tender and barely pink in center. Serve with vegetable salad, if desired. *Makes 6 servings*

NOTE: If you prefer a more moist dressing, increase chicken broth to 1½ cups.

Pork Chop with Jalapeño-Pecan Cornbread Stuffing

CREAMY PORK WITH CORNMEAL BISCUITS

2 tart green apples, peeled, cored and sliced
¼ to ½ cup onion, chopped
3 cloves garlic, minced *or*
    ¾ teaspoon garlic powder
2 teaspoons sugar
½ teaspoon dried sage
¼ teaspoon ground nutmeg
⅛ teaspoon white pepper
2 to 2½ pounds boneless pork loin, trimmed and cut into 1-inch cubes
¼ cup all-purpose flour
½ cup white cooking wine
⅓ cup whipping cream
1½ tablespoons cornstarch
Salt to taste

In CROCK-POT® Slow Cooker, combine apples, onion, garlic, sugar, sage, nutmeg and white pepper. Coat pork cubes with flour and then arrange over mixture in CROCK-POT® Slow Cooker. Pour in cooking wine. Cover and cook on Low 8 to 10 hours or on High 4 to 5 hours. Approximately 30 to 60 minutes before serving, prepare cornmeal biscuits as described below. While biscuits are baking, mix whipping cream and cornstarch in small bowl. Pour into pork mixture and stir. Increase CROCK-POT® Slow Cooker to High if it has been cooking on Low. Continue to cook until sauce is hot and bubbly. Season to taste with salt. Serve with biscuits.

Makes 6 to 8 servings

CORNMEAL BISCUITS: Preheat oven to 450°F. In large mixing bowl, stir together 1½ cups all-purpose flour, ½ cup yellow cornmeal, 1 tablespoon baking powder, 1 teaspoon sugar and ½ teaspoon salt. Dice ⅓ cup margarine. With pastry blender or 2 knives, cut margarine into flour mixture until mixture resembles coarse crumbs. Add ¾ cup plain nonfat yogurt; stir just until mixture forms a sticky dough. Form dough into ball and knead on floured surface; roll out to about ½-inch thickness. Using floured 2½-inch cutter, cut dough into 12 rounds. Place 1 inch apart on *ungreased* baking sheet. Bake 10 to 12 minutes or until golden brown. Serve hot with Creamy Pork.

Makes 12 biscuits

SPICY PORK AND CABBAGE

4 to 6 pork loin chops (about 1 inch thick), well trimmed
Salt and black pepper
Kitchen Bouquet
4 cups coarsely shredded cabbage
3 to 4 tart apples, cored and diced
½ small onion, chopped
1 cup water
¼ cup sugar
2 tablespoons cider vinegar
2 teaspoons salt
½ small bay leaf
2 whole cloves

Season pork chops lightly with salt and pepper. Brush with Kitchen Bouquet; set aside. Place cabbage, apples and onion in CROCK-POT® Slow Cooker. Add remaining ingredients except pork chops. Toss together well to evenly distribute spices. Arrange chops on top of cabbage mixture, stacking to fit. Cover and cook on Low 8 to 10 hours or on High 4 to 5 hours. Remove and discard bay leaf. *Makes 4 to 6 servings*

MEXICAN CARNITAS

1 package (10 ounces) frozen French-style green beans, partially thawed
2 tablespoons minced onion
2 tablespoons chopped pimientos
½ teaspoon seasoned salt
⅛ teaspoon black pepper
1 pound lean boneless pork, cut into small cubes

Place green beans in CROCK-POT® Slow Cooker. Top with onion, pimientos, seasoned salt and pepper; add cubed pork. Cover and cook on Low for 7 to 9 hours.

Makes 3 to 4 servings

NOTE: Double recipe for 5-quart CROCK-POT® Slow Cooker

CANTONESE SWEET AND SOUR PORK

2 pounds lean pork shoulder, cut
    into strips
1 green bell pepper, seeded and
    cut into strips
½ medium onion, thinly sliced
¼ cup packed brown sugar
2 tablespoons cornstarch
2 cups pineapple chunks,
    reserving juice
¼ cup cider vinegar
¼ cup water
1 tablespoon soy sauce
½ teaspoon salt
    Chow mein noodles

Place pork strips in CROCK-POT® Slow Cooker. Add bell pepper and onion. In bowl, mix brown sugar and cornstarch. Add 1 cup reserved pineapple juice, vinegar, water, soy sauce and salt; blend until smooth. Pour over meat and vegetables. Cover and cook on Low for 7 to 9 hours.

One hour before serving, add pineapple chunks; stir into meat and sauce.

Serve over chow mein noodles. *Makes 4 to 6 servings*

CHOP SUEY

2 to 3 pork shoulder chops,
 boned, well trimmed and
 diced
2 cups cubed, cooked or raw
 chicken
1½ cups water chestnuts, thinly
 sliced
1½ cups bamboo shoots, cut into
 julienne strips
1 cup diagonally sliced celery
½ cup chicken broth
2 teaspoons soy sauce
½ teaspoon sugar
 Salt

Combine all ingredients in CROCK-POT® Slow Cooker; stir well. Cover and cook on Low 8 to 10 hours or on High 4 to 5 hours. If desired, thicken sauce with cornstarch-water paste just before serving. *Makes 4 servings*

NOTE: Double recipe for 5-quart CROCK-POT® Slow Cooker.

STUFFED PORK CHOPS

4 double pork loin chops, well
    trimmed
  Salt and black pepper
1 can (12 ounces) whole-kernel
    corn, drained
1 small onion, chopped
1 small green bell pepper, seeded
    and chopped
1 cup fresh bread crumbs
⅓ cup uncooked long-grain
    converted rice
½ teaspoon dried oregano leaves
1 can (8 ounces) tomato sauce

Cut pocket in each chop, cutting from the edge almost to the bone. Lightly season pockets with salt and black pepper. In bowl, combine remaining ingredients except pork chops and tomato sauce. Pack vegetable mixture into pockets. Secure along fat side with wooden picks.

Pour any remaining vegetable mixture into CROCK-POT® Slow Cooker. Moisten top surface of each chop with tomato sauce. Add stuffed pork chops to CROCK-POT® Slow Cooker, stacking to fit if necessary. Pour any remaining tomato sauce on top. Cover and cook on Low 8 to 10 hours or on High 4 to 5 hours until done.

To serve, remove pork chops to heatproof platter and mound vegetable-rice mixture in center. *Makes 4 servings*

Stuffed Pork Chop

SWEET AND SOUR PORK STEAKS

4 to 6 pork shoulder steaks
1 tablespoon vegetable oil
1 can (15 ounces) crushed
    pineapple, undrained
½ cup chopped green bell pepper
½ cup water
⅓ cup packed brown sugar
2 tablespoons ketchup
1 tablespoon quick-cooking
    tapioca
1 tablespoon soy sauce
½ teaspoon dry mustard

In skillet, brown pork steaks on both sides in hot oil. Drain fat. Transfer to any size CROCK-POT® Slow Cooker.

In bowl, combine pineapple, bell pepper, water, brown sugar, ketchup, tapioca, soy sauce and mustard. Pour over pork steaks. Cover and cook on Low 8 to 10 hours or on High 4 to 5 hours. Serve over rice, if desired. *Makes 4 to 6 servings*

PORK CHOPS AND POTATOES IN MUSTARD SAUCE

6 to 8 pork loin chops
2 tablespoons vegetable oil
1 can (10¾ ounces) cream of
    mushroom soup
¼ cup chicken broth
¼ cup country Dijon-style mustard
½ teaspoon dried thyme leaves
1 clove garlic, minced *or*
    ¼ teaspoon garlic powder
¼ teaspoon black pepper
6 medium-sized potatoes, cut into
    thin slices
1 onion, sliced

In skillet, brown pork chops on both sides in hot oil. Drain fat.

In any size CROCK-POT® Slow Cooker, mix soup, chicken broth, mustard, thyme, garlic, and pepper. Add potatoes and onion, stirring to coat. Place browned pork chops on top of potato mixture. Cover and cook on Low for 8 to 10 hours or on High 4 to 5 hours.

Makes 6 servings

HAM AND CHEESE SUPPER

2 cups ground cooked ham
(about ½ pound)
½ cup finely crushed cheese
crackers
1 egg
⅓ cup barbecue sauce
4 large potatoes, peeled and
thinly sliced
1 medium onion, thinly sliced
2 tablespoons butter
2 tablespoons vegetable oil
1 cup grated mozzarella cheese
⅔ cup evaporated milk
1 teaspoon salt
¼ teaspoon paprika
⅛ teaspoon black pepper

Combine ground ham, crushed crackers, egg and barbecue sauce and shape into 6 patties. In skillet, sauté potato and onion slices in butter and oil over medium heat, turning frequently to prevent browning. Drain and place in CROCK-POT® Slow Cooker.

Combine cheese, milk and seasonings and pour over potatoes and onions. Layer ham patties on top. Cover and cook on Low for 3 to 5 hours. *Makes 6 servings*

Ham and Cheese Supper

BAKED HAM WITH MUSTARD GLAZE

3 to 5 pounds precooked ham, drained
10 to 12 whole cloves
½ cup packed brown sugar
1 tablespoon prepared mustard
2 teaspoons lemon juice
2 tablespoons orange juice
2 tablespoons cornstarch

Score ham in diamond pattern and stud with cloves. Place in CROCK-POT® Slow Cooker. Combine brown sugar, mustard and lemon juice; spoon over ham. Cover and cook on High 1 hour, then on Low 6 to 7 hours or until ham is hot.

Remove ham to warm serving platter. Turn CROCK-POT® Slow Cooker to High setting. Combine orange juice and cornstarch to form smooth paste. Stir into drippings in CROCK-POT® Slow Cooker. Cook stirring occasionally until sauce is thickened. Spoon over ham. *Makes 12 to 15 servings*

NOTE: If using 5- or 6-quart CROCK-POT® and cooking larger ham, cook 1 hour on High, then Low 8 to 10 hours.

HAM TETRAZZINI

- 1 to 1½ cups cubed cooked ham
- 1 can (10¾ ounces) condensed cream of mushroom soup
- 1 can (4 ounces) sliced mushrooms, drained
- ½ cup grated Romano or Parmesan cheese
- ½ cup stuffed olives, sliced (optional)
- ½ cup evaporated or scalded milk
- ¼ cup dry sherry or dry white wine
- 1½ teaspoons prepared horseradish
- 1 package (5 ounces) spaghetti
- 2 tablespoons butter, melted

Combine all ingredients except spaghetti and butter in CROCK-POT® Slow Cooker; stir well. Cover and cook on Low for 6 to 8 hours.

Just before serving, cook spaghetti according to package directions; drain and toss with butter. Stir into CROCK-POT® Slow Cooker. Sprinkle additional grated cheese over top.

Makes 4 servings

NOTE: This recipe may be doubled for the 5-quart CROCK-POT® Slow Cooker.

FRUIT AND HAM LOAF

¾ **cup dried fruit bits**
2 **tablespoons apple butter**
1 **pound ground, fully cooked ham**
½ **pound ground pork**
½ **cup graham cracker crumbs**
¼ **cup milk**
1 **beaten egg**
½ **teaspoon black pepper**
½ **cup packed brown sugar**
2 **tablespoons apple juice**
½ **teaspoon dry mustard**

In small bowl, combine fruit bits and apple butter. In large bowl, combine ham, pork, graham cracker crumbs, milk, egg and pepper.

Crisscross 3 foil strips as described on page 7 (atop a sheet of waxed paper to keep counter clean). In center of foil strips pat half of meat mixture into 7-inch circle. Spread fruit mixture on meat circle to within 1 inch of edges. Top with remaining meat mixture. Press edges of meat to seal well. Bringing up foil strips, lift and transfer to any size CROCK-POT® Slow Cooker. Press meat away from sides of CROCK-POT® Slow Cooker to avoid excess browning. Cover and cook on Low 8 to 10 hours or on High 4 to 6 hours. Loaf is done when meat thermometer inserted reads 170°F.

In small bowl, combine brown sugar, apple juice and mustard. Spread over meat. Cover and cook on Low or High heat 30 minutes more.

Using foil strips, lift ham loaf from CROCK-POT® Slow Cooker and transfer to serving plate; discard foil strips. Serve.

Makes 6 to 8 servings

LAMB SHANKS WITH SPLIT PEAS

   1 cup dried split green peas
   3 pounds lamb shanks
2½ cups beef broth
   1 large onion, chopped
   2 carrots, peeled and sliced
   2 stalks celery, sliced
     Salt and black pepper

To soften peas, cover with 3 times their volume of unsalted water and bring to a boil. Boil 10 minutes, reduce heat, cover and allow to simmer 1½ hours or until peas are tender. Brown lamb shanks under broiler to remove fat; drain well. Mix all ingredients except shanks in CROCK-POT® Slow Cooker; stir well. Add shanks, pushing down into liquid. Cover and cook on Low 10 to 12 hours.

Makes 4 to 6 servings

LAMB CHOPS WITH ORANGE SAUCE

   8 lamb rib chops
   2 tablespoons vegetable oil
½ cup orange juice
   2 tablespoons honey
   2 tablespoons cornstarch
   2 teaspoons salt
   1 teaspoon grated orange peel

In large skillet, brown lamb chops in oil; drain well. Thoroughly combine orange juice, honey, cornstarch, salt and grated orange peel. Brush browned lamb chops with orange mixture and place in CROCK-POT® Slow Cooker. Cover and cook on Low 6 to 8 hours.

If thicker sauce is desired, remove chops before serving and turn CROCK-POT® Slow Cooker to High; stir in mixture of 2 tablespoons cornstarch and ¼ cup water. Cook, stirring, until sauce is transparent.

Makes 4 servings

CANDIED POLYNESIAN SPARERIBS

2 pounds lean pork spareribs
$\frac{1}{3}$ cup soy sauce
$\frac{1}{4}$ cup cornstarch
1 tablespoon ground ginger
1 cup sugar
$\frac{1}{2}$ cup cider vinegar
$\frac{1}{4}$ cup water
1 teaspoon salt
$\frac{1}{2}$ teaspoon dry mustard
1 small piece gingerroot or crystallized ginger (about 1 inch long)

Cut spareribs into individual 3-inch pieces. Mix soy sauce, cornstarch and ground ginger until smooth; brush mixture over spareribs. Place ribs on rack of broiler pan. Bake in preheated 425°F oven 20 minutes to remove fat; drain. Combine remaining ingredients in CROCK-POT® Slow Cooker; stir well. Add browned ribs. Cover and cook on Low 8 to 10 hours or on High 4 to 5 hours.

If desired, brown and crisp ribs in broiler for 10 minutes before serving.
Makes 4 servings

MAIN DISHES

BRAISED SHORT RIBS

3 to 4 pounds lean beef short ribs
½ cup all-purpose flour
1½ teaspoons paprika
1 teaspoon salt
½ teaspoon dry mustard
2 medium onions, sliced and
   separated into rings
1 cup beer, beef broth or water
1 clove garlic, chopped (optional)
3 tablespoons water (optional)
2 tablespoons all-purpose flour
   (optional)

Place short ribs on broiler rack or in skillet; brown to remove fat. Drain well. Combine ½ cup flour, paprika, salt and mustard; toss with short ribs. Add rib mixture to CROCK-POT® Slow Cooker. Place onions, beer and garlic in CROCK-POT® Slow Cooker; stir to mix beef ribs with onion rings (be sure onions are under beef ribs—not on top). Cover and cook on Low 8 to 12 hours or on High 4 to 6 hours.

Remove short ribs to warm serving platter. If thickened gravy is desired, make a smooth paste with 2 tablespoons flour and water. Turn CROCK-POT® Slow Cooker to High and stir in paste. Cover and cook until gravy is thickened. *Makes 6 servings*

HONEY RIBS AND RICE

2 pounds extra-lean back ribs
1 can (10½ ounces) condensed
   beef consommé
½ cup water
3 tablespoons soy sauce
2 tablespoons maple syrup
2 tablespoons honey
2 tablespoons barbecue sauce
½ teaspoon dry mustard
1½ cups quick cooking rice

If ribs are fat, place on broiler rack and broil for 15 to 20 minutes; drain well. Otherwise, wash ribs and pat dry. Cut ribs into single servings. Combine remaining ingredients except rice in CROCK-POT® Slow Cooker; stir to mix. Add ribs. Cover and cook on Low for 8 to 10 hours or on High for 4 to 5 hours.

Remove ribs and keep warm. Turn CROCK-POT® Slow Cooker to High setting; add rice and cook until done.

Serve rice on warm platter surrounded by ribs.

Makes 4 servings

221

SPARERIBS SIMMERED IN ORANGE SAUCE

4 pounds country-style pork spareribs

2 tablespoons vegetable oil

2 medium white onions, cut into ¼-inch slices

1 to 2 tablespoons dried ancho chilies, seeded and finely chopped

½ teaspoon ground cinnamon

¼ teaspoon ground cloves

1 can (16 ounces) tomatoes, undrained

2 cloves garlic

½ cup orange juice

⅓ cup dry white wine

⅓ cup packed brown sugar

1 teaspoon shredded orange peel

½ teaspoon salt

1 to 2 tablespoons cider vinegar
Orange wedges (optional)

Trim excess fat from ribs. Cut into individual riblets. Heat oil in large skillet over medium heat. Add ribs; cook 10 minutes or until browned on all sides. Remove to plate. Remove and discard all but 2 tablespoons drippings from skillet. Add onions, chilies, cinnamon and cloves. Cook and stir 4 minutes or until softened. Transfer onion mixture to slow cooker.

Process tomatoes with juice and garlic in food processor or blender until smooth.

Combine tomato mixture, orange juice, wine, sugar, orange peel and salt in slow cooker. Add ribs; stir to coat. Cover and cook on Low 5 hours or until ribs are fork-tender. Remove ribs to plates. Ladle out liquid to medium bowl. Let stand 5 minutes. Skim and discard fat. Stir in vinegar; serve over ribs. Serve with carrots and garnish with orange wedges, if desired. *Makes 4 to 6 servings*

Spareribs Simmered in Orange Sauce

MEATBALL GRINDERS

1 can (15 ounces) diced tomatoes, drained and juices reserved

1 can (8 ounces) reduced-sodium tomato sauce

¼ cup chopped onion

2 tablespoons tomato paste

1 teaspoon dried Italian seasoning

1 pound ground chicken

½ cup fresh whole wheat or white bread crumbs (1 slice bread)

1 egg white, lightly beaten

3 tablespoons finely chopped fresh parsley

2 cloves garlic, minced

¼ teaspoon salt

⅛ teaspoon black pepper

4 small hard rolls, split

2 tablespoons grated Parmesan cheese

Combine diced tomatoes, ½ cup reserved juice, tomato sauce, onion, tomato paste and Italian seasoning in slow cooker. Cover and cook on Low 3 to 4 hours or until onions are soft.

During the last 30 minutes of cooking time, prepare meatballs. Combine chicken, bread crumbs, egg white, parsley, garlic, salt and pepper in medium bowl. With wet hands form mixture into 12 to 16 meatballs. Spray medium nonstick skillet with cooking spray; heat over medium heat until hot. Add meatballs; cook about 8 to 10 minutes or until well-browned on all sides. Remove meatballs to slow cooker; cook 1 to 2 hours or until meatballs are no longer pink in centers and are heated through.

Place 3 to 4 meatballs in each roll. Divide sauce evenly; spoon over meatballs. Sprinkle with cheese. *Makes 4 servings*

Meatball Grinder

SLOPPY JOES

3 pounds ground beef
1 cup chopped onion
2 cloves garlic, minced *or*
  ¼ teaspoon garlic powder
1½ cups ketchup
1 cup chopped green bell pepper
½ cup water
4 tablespoons brown sugar
4 tablespoons prepared mustard
4 tablespoons vinegar
4 tablespoons Worcestershire
  sauce
3 teaspoons chili powder
Hamburger buns

In large skillet, brown ground beef, onion and garlic. Cook until meat is brown and onion is tender. Drain fat.

In any size CROCK-POT® Slow Cooker, combine ketchup, bell pepper, water, brown sugar, mustard, vinegar, Worcestershire sauce and chili powder. Stir in meat mixture. Cover and cook on Low 6 to 8 hours or on High 3 to 4 hours. Spoon into hamburger buns. *Makes 8 to 10 servings*

VARIATION: Substitute ground turkey, chicken or pork for the ground beef.

MAIN DISHES

PEPPERED MEAT LOAF

2 pounds ground chuck
½ pound bulk sausage
1 large onion, finely chopped
1 can (8 ounces) tomato sauce
¾ cup crushed saltine crackers
½ cup ketchup
2 eggs
3 cloves garlic, minced
2 teaspoons Worcestershire sauce
1 teaspoon seasoned salt
¼ teaspoon seasoned black pepper
1 to 2 potatoes, peeled and cut
   into fingers
Sauce (recipe follows)

Combine all ingredients except potatoes and Sauce in large bowl; mix well and shape into loaf. Place potatoes in bottom of CROCK-POT® Slow Cooker. Top potatoes with meat loaf. Pour Sauce over top. Cover and cook on Low 8 to 12 hours.

Makes 6 to 8 servings

SAUCE

1 cup ketchup
⅓ cup packed brown sugar
1½ teaspoons dry mustard
½ teaspoon nutmeg

Mix ingredients together in small bowl.

BEEF 'N' BEAN BURRITOS

3 cups water
1 can (12 ounces) tomato paste
2 packages (1½ ounces each)
    enchilada sauce mix
¼ teaspoon black pepper
⅛ teaspoon garlic powder
    Salt to taste
2 pounds ground beef
1 can (12 ounces) refried beans
5 (9-inch) flour tortillas
4 cups shredded Cheddar cheese

Lightly grease CROCK-POT® Slow Cooker. In CROCK-POT® Slow Cooker, place foil handles (see page 7). Combine water, tomato paste, enchilada sauce mix, black pepper, garlic powder and salt in medium saucepan; simmer 15 minutes over low heat. Brown ground beef in large skillet; drain. Stir in ⅓ of sauce mix into browned beef. Spoon small amount of sauce into bottom of CROCK-POT® Slow Cooker. Spread small amount of refried beans over flour tortilla. Place tortilla on top of sauce in CROCK-POT® Slow Cooker, tearing to fit if necessary. Spoon ¼ of meat mixture over tortilla and then top with small amount of cheese. Continue layering process until top of CROCK-POT® Slow Cooker is reached, ending with layer of cheese. Cover and cook on Low 6 to 8 hours or on High 3 to 4 hours. Lift burritos out by foil handles and place on serving plate. Cut in wedges and garnish with taco sauce, sour cream, salsa, chopped onion, chili peppers and guacamole. *Makes 4 to 6 servings*

NORWEGIAN MEATBALLS IN SAUCE

1½ pounds extra-lean ground beef
½ pound extra-lean ground pork or veal
1 cup mashed potatoes
½ cup dry bread crumbs
½ cup milk
1 egg
1 teaspoon seasoned salt
¼ teaspoon ground ginger
¼ teaspoon ground nutmeg
¼ teaspoon ground allspice
¼ teaspoon ground cloves
¼ teaspoon black pepper
¼ teaspoon brown sugar
½ cup all-purpose flour
1 cup beef broth
½ cup heavy cream
½ cup chopped parsley

Thoroughly combine all ingredients except flour, beef broth, heavy cream and chopped parsley. Blend well and shape into about twenty-four 1½-inch meatballs. Roll lightly in flour. Place on rack of broiler pan in preheated 400°F oven 20 minutes. Drain and place in CROCK-POT® Slow Cooker. Pour beef broth over meatballs. Cover and cook on Low 7 to 9 hours or on High 2 to 3 hours.

Before serving, carefully remove meatballs to warm platter. Stir heavy cream into broth in CROCK-POT® Slow Cooker; mix until smooth. Pour sauce over meatballs, then sprinkle with chopped parsley. *Makes 6 to 8 servings*

CURRY BEEF

1 pound lean ground beef
½ cup beef broth
1 medium onion, thinly sliced
1 tablespoon curry powder
1 teaspoon ground cumin
2 cloves garlic, minced
1 cup (8 ounces) sour cream
¼ cup reduced-fat (2%) milk
½ cup raisins, divided
1 teaspoon sugar
12 ounces wide egg noodles *or*
    1⅓ cups long-grain white rice
¼ cup chopped walnuts, almonds
    or pecans

Heat large skillet over high heat. Add beef, cook until browned; pour off fat.

Add beef broth, onion, curry powder, cumin, garlic and cooked beef to slow cooker. Cover and cook on Low 4 hours. Stir in sour cream, milk, ¼ cup raisins and sugar. Cover and cook 30 minutes or until thickened and heated through.

Cook noodles according to package directions; drain. Spoon beef curry over noodles. Sprinkle remaining ¼ cup raisins and walnuts over beef curry. *Makes 4 servings*

SERVING SUGGESTION: Serve with sliced cucumber sprinkled with sugar and vinegar or plain yogurt topped with brown sugar, chopped bananas and green onions.

Curry Beef

SPANISH–STYLE COUSCOUS

1 pound lean ground beef
1 can (about 14 ounces) beef broth
1 small green bell pepper, cut into ½-inch pieces
½ cup pimiento-stuffed green olives, sliced
½ medium onion, chopped
2 cloves garlic, minced
1 teaspoon ground cumin
½ teaspoon dried thyme leaves
1 cup couscous

Heat skillet over high heat until hot. Add beef; cook until browned. Pour off fat. Place broth, bell pepper, olives, onion, garlic, cumin, thyme and beef in slow cooker. Cook on Low 4 hours or until bell pepper is tender.

Bring 1⅓ cups water to a boil over high heat in 1-quart saucepan. Stir in couscous. Cover; remove from heat. Let stand 5 minutes; fluff with fork. Spoon couscous onto plates; top with beef mixture.

Makes 4 servings

SERVING SUGGESTION: Serve with carrot sticks.

SWEET AND SOUR MEATBALLS OVER RICE

1 pound ground beef
1 egg, lightly beaten
4 tablespoons cornstarch, divided
1 tablespoon dried chopped onion
1 teaspoon salt
$\frac{1}{4}$ teaspoon black pepper
1 tablespoon vegetable oil
1 large green bell pepper, cut into pieces
$\frac{1}{2}$ cup sugar
3 tablespoons vinegar
1 tablespoon soy sauce
1 can (15 ounces) pineapple chunks, drained
Hot cooked rice

In large bowl, combine ground beef, egg, 1 tablespoon cornstarch, onion, salt and pepper. Shape into 1½-inch balls. In large skillet, lightly brown meatballs in oil. Drain fat from skillet. Transfer meatballs to any size CROCK-POT® Slow Cooker.

Stir together bell pepper, sugar, vinegar, remaining cornstarch and soy sauce. Pour over meatballs. Cover and cook on Low 6 to 8 hours or on High 2 to 4 hours. In last 30 minutes of cooking, stir in pineapple. Serve over hot cooked rice.

Makes 4 to 5 servings

VARIATION: Substitute ground turkey for ground beef.

233

MEAT LOAF ITALIAN–STYLE

1 can (8 ounces) pizza sauce, divided
1 beaten egg
½ cup chopped onion
½ cup chopped green bell pepper
⅓ cup dry seasoned bread crumbs
½ teaspoon garlic salt
¼ teaspoon black pepper
1½ pounds ground beef
1 cup shredded mozzarella cheese

Reserve ⅓ cup pizza sauce; cover and refrigerate. In bowl, combine remaining pizza sauce and egg. Stir in onion, bell pepper, bread crumbs, garlic salt and black pepper. Add ground beef and mix well.

Form meat mixture into a loaf and place on 3 strips of foil as described on Page 7. Transfer loaf to any size CROCK-POT® Slow Cooker. Cover and cook on Low 8 to 10 hours or on High 4 to 6 hours. To ensure doneness, insert meat thermometer into center of loaf; internal temperature should read 170°F.

Spread loaf with reserved ⅓ cup pizza sauce. Sprinkle with cheese. Cover and let cook 15 minutes more or until cheese is melted. Using foil strips, lift loaf from CROCK-POT® Slow Cooker and transfer to serving plate. Discard foil strips. Serve.

Makes 8 servings

Meat Loaf Italian-Style

TACO BAKE

1 pound ground beef
1 onion, chopped
1 can (15 ounces) tomato sauce
¾ cup water
1 package (1¼ ounces) taco seasoning
1 package (8 ounces) shell macaroni, uncooked
1 can (4 ounces) mild chopped green chilies
2 cups mild shredded Cheddar cheese

In large skillet, brown ground beef and onion; drain fat. Add tomato sauce, water and taco seasoning; mix. Simmer 20 minutes. Transfer to CROCK-POT® Slow Cooker. Stir in macaroni and chopped green chilies. Cover and cook on Low 6 to 8 hours or on High 3 to 4 hours. In last 30 minutes of cooking, top with cheese.

Makes 6 to 8 servings

TOSTADA PIE

1½ cups chopped onions
  2 teaspoons vegetable oil or olive oil
  2 pounds ground beef
  1 teaspoon chili powder
  1 teaspoon ground cumin
  1 teaspoon salt
  2 cloves garlic, minced *or*
    ¼ teaspoon garlic powder
  1 can (16 ounces) tomato sauce
  1 cup sliced black olives
    Soft margarine or butter
  8 corn tortillas
  4 cups shredded Monterey Jack cheese

Sauté onions in skillet in hot oil. Add ground beef, chili powder, cumin, salt and garlic. When ground beef is brown, stir in tomato sauce. Heat through. Stir in black olives.

Prepare foil strips as directed on page 7. Place in any size CROCK-POT® Slow Cooker. Lightly butter one corn tortilla. Lay one tortilla, buttered side up, on foil strips. Spread with meat sauce and layer of cheese. Cover with another tortilla, more meat sauce and cheese. Repeat layers ending with cheese. Cover; cook on High 1 hour. When ready to serve, lift out using foil strips and transfer to serving dish. Discard foil strips. Cut into wedges. Serve with sour cream and green onion, if desired.

Makes 4 to 5 servings

MAIN DISHES

SUZIE'S SLOPPY JOES

3 pounds lean ground beef
1 cup chopped onion
3 cloves garlic, minced
1¼ cups ketchup
1 cup chopped red bell pepper
5 tablespoons Worcestershire sauce
4 tablespoons brown sugar
3 tablespoons prepared mustard
3 tablespoons cider vinegar
2 teaspoons chili powder
Hamburger buns

Brown ground beef, onion, and garlic in very large skillet. Drain excess fat.

Combine ketchup, bell pepper, Worcestershire sauce, brown sugar, mustard, vinegar and chili powder in slow cooker. Stir in beef mixture. Cover and cook on Low 6 to 8 hours. Spoon into hamburger buns.

Makes 8 to 10 servings

MEATBALLS WITH GRAVY

1½ pounds ground beef
¼ cup bread crumbs
¼ cup milk
1 egg
2 tablespoons chopped parsley
1 teaspoon onion salt
¼ teaspoon garlic powder
2 packages brown gravy mix

Combine all ingredients, except gravy mix, to form mixture into 1-inch meatballs. Brown in skillet. Drain fat. Place in CROCK-POT® Slow Cooker. Cover. Cook on Low 3 to 4 hours or can be kept on all day. When ready to serve, prepare gravy mix as directed on package and pour into meatballs. Stir. Serve over rice, if desired.

Makes 6 servings

Suzie's Sloppy Joes

BURGER 'N' BEAN HOT DISH

1 pound ground beef
1 can (16 ounces) barbecue beans
1 can (11½ ounces) condensed
    bean with bacon soup
1 tablespoon instant minced onion
½ teaspoon garlic salt
¼ teaspoon chili powder
⅛ teaspoon seasoned black pepper
½ cup grated processed American
    cheese

In skillet, brown ground beef; drain well. Thoroughly combine all ingredients except cheese in CROCK-POT® Slow Cooker. Cover and cook on Low 6 to 9 hours.

Just before serving, sprinkle with grated cheese. Serve over hot corn bread, if desired. *Makes 6 servings*

ZESTY MEATBALL SANDWICHES

1 egg
2 cloves garlic, minced *or*
      ¼ teaspoon garlic powder
½ teaspoon salt
½ teaspoon Italian seasoning
¼ teaspoon red pepper flakes
1 pound ground beef
1 pound ground turkey
½ cup bread crumbs
⅓ cup grated Parmesan cheese
¼ cup chopped onion
1 can (16 ounces) tomato sauce
2 tablespoons red wine vinegar
6 to 8 hoagie-type sandwich rolls,
    split and warmed
  Condiments, if desired:
    shredded mozzarella cheese,
    red and yellow bell pepper
    strips, sliced onion, olives

In large bowl, beat egg, garlic, salt, Italian seasoning and red pepper flakes. Add beef, turkey, bread crumbs, Parmesan cheese and onion; mix well. Shape mixture into 1-inch balls and brown in large skillet. Drain meatballs and transfer to 5-quart CROCK-POT® Slow Cooker.

In same bowl, mix tomato sauce and vinegar; pour over meatballs. Cover and cook on Low 5½ to 6 hours.

To serve, place 3 to 4 meatballs in each split roll; top with sauce from CROCK-POT® Slow Cooker. If desired, add condiments and serve. *Makes 6 to 8 servings*

STUFFED CABBAGE

12 large cabbage leaves
 4 cups water
 1 pound lean ground beef or lamb
½ cup cooked rice
½ teaspoon salt
¼ teaspoon dried thyme leaves
¼ teaspoon ground nutmeg
¼ teaspoon ground cinnamon
⅛ teaspoon black pepper
 1 can (6 ounces) tomato paste
¾ cup water

Wash cabbage leaves. Boil 4 cups water. Turn heat off. Soak leaves in water 5 minutes. Remove, drain and cool.

Combine remaining ingredients except tomato paste and ¾ cup water. Place 2 tablespoons beef mixture on each cabbage leaf and roll firmly. Stack in CROCK-POT® Slow Cooker. Combine tomato paste and ¾ cup water and pour over stuffed cabbage. Cover and cook on Low 8 to 10 hours.   *Makes 6 servings*

HAMBURGER HOT POT

1½ pounds ground chuck or lean
      ground beef
 1 teaspoon salt
¼ teaspoon garlic powder
¼ teaspoon black pepper
 6 medium potatoes, peeled and
      sliced
 3 medium onions, sliced
 1 can (10¾ ounces) condensed
      golden mushroom soup
½ cup water

In skillet, lightly brown ground beef; drain well. Add salt, garlic powder and pepper; set aside. Place half of potatoes and half of onions in greased CROCK-POT® Slow Cooker. Add browned beef. Top with remaining potatoes and onions. Combine mushroom soup and water; spread over top, being sure to moisten and cover evenly. Cover and cook on Low 8 to 10 hours or on High 3 to 4 hours.   *Makes 4 to 6 servings*

Stuffed Cabbage

FEIJOADA COMPLETA

1½ pounds country-style ribs or
  pork spareribs
1 corned beef (1½ pounds)
½ pound smoked link sausage,
  such as Polish or andouille
½ pound fresh link sausage, such
  as bratwurst or breakfast links
3 cups water
1 can (15½ ounces) black beans,
  rinsed and drained
1 cup chopped onion
4 cloves garlic, minced
1 jalapeño pepper,* seeded and
  chopped
  Chili-Lemon Sauce (recipe
  follows)

Trim excess fat from ribs. Combine all ingredients except Chili-Lemon Sauce in slow cooker; stir to mix well. Cover and cook on Low 7 to 8 hours or until meats are fork-tender. Meanwhile, prepare Chili-Lemon Sauce.

Remove meats to cutting board. Slice corned beef; place on large serving platter. Arrange remaining meat around corned beef. Cover meat and keep warm.

Drain liquid from beans, leaving just enough liquid so beans are moist. Transfer to serving bowl. Serve with Chili-Lemon Sauce.

Makes 10 to 12 servings

CHILI–LEMON SAUCE
  ¾ cup lemon juice
  1 small onion, coarsely chopped
  3 jalapeño peppers,* seeded and chopped
  3 cloves garlic, cut into halves

*Jalapeño peppers can sting and irritate the skin; wear rubber gloves when handling peppers and do not touch eyes.

Place all ingredients in food processor or blender. Process until smooth. Serve at room temperature.

Makes about 1 cup

Feijoada Completa

MAIN DISHES

SAUSAGE–RICE CASSEROLE

1 pound bulk sausage
4 cups water
2 stalks celery, diced
¾ cup uncooked long-grain converted rice
⅓ cup slivered almonds
1 envelope (1½ ounces) dry chicken soup mix
Salt to taste

In skillet, brown sausage; drain well. Combine all ingredients in lightly greased CROCK-POT® Slow Cooker; stir well. Cover and cook on Low 7 to 10 hours or on High 3 to 4 hours or until rice is tender.

Makes 4 servings

CAMP–OUT CHILI DOGS

2 cans (15 ounces each) chili with beans
1 pound frankfurters
1 large onion, finely chopped *or* 3 tablespoons dried minced onion
1 teaspoon chili powder
¼ pound Cheddar cheese, cubed or grated
Frankfurter rolls

Combine all ingredients except cheese and rolls in CROCK-POT® Slow Cooker. Stir well. Cover and cook on Low 5 to 10 hours or on High 2 to 3 hours.

Add cheese just before serving and allow to melt slightly. Serve each frankfurter in a roll and spoon sauce over top.

Makes 6 to 8 servings

Sausage-Rice Casserole

SAUSAGE BEAN QUICKIE

4 to 6 cooked brown 'n' serve
    sausage links, cut into 1-inch
    pieces
2 cans (16 ounces each) red
    kidney or baked beans,
    drained
1 can (7 ounces) pineapple
    chunks, undrained
2 teaspoons cider vinegar
2 teaspoons brown sugar
3 tablespoons all-purpose flour

Combine sausage, beans, pineapple and vinegar in CROCK-POT® Slow Cooker. Mix brown sugar with flour and add; stir well. Cover and cook on Low for 7 to 10 hours or on High for 2 to 3 hours.

Makes 4 servings

SALMON–WICHES

1 can (16 ounces) salmon,
  drained and flaked
1 cup dry bread crumbs
2 eggs
½ teaspoon celery salt
¼ teaspoon dried thyme leaves
1 cup crushed cheese crackers
  Vegetable oil
3 English muffins, split, toasted
  and buttered
2 cups Hollandaise sauce
  Paprika

In bowl, combine salmon, bread crumbs, eggs, celery salt and thyme. Shape into 6 patties and coat well with crushed crackers. In skillet, sauté patties in hot oil; drain. Transfer to CROCK-POT® Slow Cooker. Cover and cook on High 2 to 3 hours. Place one patty on each English muffin half and top with Hollandaise. Sprinkle with paprika.   *Makes 6 servings*

CHINESE CASHEW TUNA

1 can (16 ounces) bean sprouts, drained
1 can (10¾ ounces) condensed cream of mushroom soup
1 cup diced celery
1 cup cashew nuts, coarsely chopped
1 can (7 ounces) tuna, drained and flaked
½ cup minced onion
3 tablespoons margarine
1 tablespoon soy sauce
1 can (5½ ounces) chow mein noodles

Combine all ingredients except chow mein noodles in CROCK-POT® Slow Cooker; stir well. Cover and cook on Low 5 to 9 hours or on High 2 to 3 hours.

Serve over chow mein noodles.   *Makes 4 servings*

CHINESE CASHEW CHICKEN: Substitute 1 cup diced cooked chicken for tuna.

EASY SHRIMP CREOLE

2 tablespoons butter or margarine
$\frac{1}{3}$ cup chopped onion
2 tablespoons buttermilk biscuit
   mix
$1\frac{1}{2}$ cups water
1 can (6 ounces) tomato paste
$\frac{1}{2}$ cup chopped celery
$\frac{1}{2}$ cup chopped green bell pepper
1 teaspoon salt
$\frac{1}{4}$ teaspoon sugar
1 bay leaf
   Dash black pepper
2 pounds frozen shrimp, thawed,
   peeled and cleaned *or* 3 cans
   (5 ounces each) shrimp,
   rinsed and drained
   Hot cooked rice

In skillet, melt butter; add onion and cook slightly. Add biscuit mix and stir until well blended. Combine remaining ingredients except shrimp and rice. Add with onion mixture to CROCK-POT® Slow Cooker; stir well. Cover and cook on Low 7 to 9 hours.

One hour before serving, turn to High and add shrimp. Remove bay leaf and serve over rice. *Makes 6 servings*

NOTE: Double recipe for 5-quart CROCK-POT® Slow Cooker.

HALIBUT IN CREAMY WINE SAUCE

2 packages (12 ounces each)
   frozen halibut steaks, thawed
2 tablespoons all-purpose flour
1 tablespoon sugar
1/4 teaspoon salt
1/4 cup butter
2/3 cup milk or half-and-half
1/3 cup dry white wine
   Lemon wedges

Pat halibut steaks dry; place in CROCK-POT® Slow Cooker. Combine flour, sugar and salt.

In saucepan, melt butter; stir in flour mixture. When well blended, add milk and wine; cook over medium heat until thickened, stirring constantly. Allow sauce to boil 1 minute while stirring. Pour sauce over fish. Cover and cook on High 2½ to 3 hours.

Transfer halibut to serving platter; garnish with lemon.

Makes 6 servings

HERBED SALMON BAKE

2 chicken bouillon cubes
1 cup boiling water
1 can (16 ounces) salmon,
   drained and flaked
2 cups seasoned stuffing croutons
1 cup (4 ounces) shredded
   Cheddar cheese
2 eggs, beaten
1/4 teaspoon dry mustard

Dissolve bouillon cubes in boiling water. Combine all ingredients; mix well. Pour into well-greased CROCK-POT® Slow Cooker. Cover and cook on High 2 to 4 hours. *Makes 4 servings*

SWISS–CRAB CASEROLE

3 tablespoons butter
½ cup chopped celery
½ cup chopped onion
¼ cup chopped green bell pepper (optional)
3 tablespoons all-purpose flour
3 chicken bouillon cubes
2½ cups boiling water
2 cans (7 ounces each) crabmeat, drained, flaked and cartilage removed
2 cups (8 ounces) shredded Swiss cheese
1 cup quick-cooking rice
1 can (4 ounces) sliced mushrooms, drained
¼ cup sliced pimiento-stuffed olives
¼ cup sliced almonds (optional)
1 cup buttered bread crumbs
½ cup shredded Swiss cheese

In skillet, melt butter and lightly sauté celery, onion and bell pepper. Remove from heat and blend in flour. Dissolve bouillon cubes in boiling water. Add to skillet and bring to a boil, stirring constantly. Cook sauce over medium heat about 2 minutes or until slightly thickened.

Lightly toss remaining ingredients except buttered crumbs and ½ cup shredded cheese in CROCK-POT® Slow Cooker. Add sauce; stir lightly to blend. Cover and cook on High 3 to 5 hours.

Pour contents of CROCK-POT® Slow Cooker into shallow heatproof serving dish. Cover with buttered bread crumbs and sprinkle with ½ cup shredded cheese. Set under broiler until cheese is melted and bread crumbs are crunchy brown.

Makes 4 to 6 servings

JAMBALAYA

1 can (28 ounces) whole tomatoes
2 cups diced boiled ham
2 medium onions, coarsely
    chopped
1 cup uncooked long-grain
    converted rice
2 stalks celery, sliced
½ green bell pepper, seeded and
    diced
¼ cup tomato paste
2 tablespoons vegetable oil
3 cloves garlic, minced
1 tablespoon minced parsley
½ teaspoon dried thyme leaves
2 whole cloves
1 pound fresh or frozen shrimp,
    peeled and deviened

Thoroughly mix all ingredients except shrimp in CROCK-POT® Slow Cooker. Cover and cook on Low 8 to 10 hours.

One hour before serving, turn CROCK-POT® Slow Cooker to High. Stir in uncooked shrimp. Cover and cook until shrimp are pink and tender.
Makes 4 to 6 servings

Jambalaya

SWEET–AND–SOUR SHRIMP

1 package (6 ounces) frozen Chinese pea pods, partially thawed
1 can (13 ounces) juice-packed pineapple chunks or tidbits, drain and reserve ½ cup juice
3 tablespoons sugar
2 tablespoons cornstarch
1 chicken bouillon cube
1 cup boiling water
2 teaspoons soy sauce
½ teaspoon ground ginger
2 cans (4½ ounces each) shrimp, rinsed and drained
2 tablespoons cider vinegar
  Hot cooked rice

Place pea pods and drained pineapple in CROCK-POT® Slow Cooker. In small saucepan, stir together sugar and cornstarch. Dissolve bouillon cube in boiling water and add with reserved pineapple juice, soy sauce and ginger to saucepan. Bring to a boil, stirring constantly. Cook sauce about 1 minute or until thickened and transparent. Gently blend sauce into pea pods and pineapple. Cover and cook on Low 5 to 6 hours.

Before serving, add shrimp and vinegar, stirring carefully to avoid breaking up shrimp. Serve over hot rice.

Makes 4 to 5 servings

MAIN DISHES

CLAM CASSEROLE

3 cans (6½ ounces each) minced
    clams, drained
18 saltine crackers, coarsely
    crushed (about 1 cup)
4 eggs, well beaten
½ cup minced onion
⅓ cup milk
¼ cup butter, melted
¼ cup minced green bell pepper
1 teaspoon salt

In bowl, mix all ingredients. Pour into well-greased CROCK-POT® Slow Cooker. Cover and cook on Low 5 to 6 hours.

Makes 6 servings

SALMON AND POTATO CASSEROLE

4 potatoes, peeled and thinly
    sliced
3 tablespoons all-purpose flour
  Salt and black pepper
1 can (16 ounces) salmon,
    drained and flaked
1 medium onion, chopped
1 can (10¾ ounces) cream of
    mushroom soup
¼ cup water
  Ground nutmeg

Place half of potatoes in greased CROCK-POT® Slow Cooker. Sprinkle with half of flour, salt and pepper. Cover with half of salmon; sprinkle with half of onion. Repeat layers in order.

Combine soup and water. Pour over potato-salmon mixture. Dust with nutmeg. Cover and cook on Low 7 to 10 hours.

Makes 6 servings

TUNA SALAD CASSEROLE

2 cans (7 ounces each) tuna,
   drained and flaked
1½ cups diced celery
1½ cups crushed potato chips,
   divided
1 can (10¾ ounces) condensed
   cream of celery soup
3 hard-cooked eggs, chopped
½ cup mayonnaise
¼ teaspoon black pepper

Combine all ingredients except ¼ cup crushed potato chips; stir well. Pour into greased CROCK-POT® Slow Cooker. Top with reserved potato chips. Cover and cook on Low 5 to 8 hours.

Makes 4 servings

Tuna Salad Casserole

BEAN AND CORNBREAD CASSEROLE

1 onion, chopped
1 green bell pepper, chopped
2 cloves garlic, minced
1 can (16 ounces) red kidney beans, undrained
1 can (16 ounces) pinto beans, undrained
1 can (16 ounces) no-salt-added diced tomatoes, undrained
1 can (8 ounces) no-salt-added tomato sauce
1 teaspoon chili powder
½ teaspoon black pepper
½ teaspoon prepared mustard
⅛ teaspoon hot sauce
1 cup yellow cornmeal
1 cup all-purpose flour
2½ teaspoons baking powder
1 tablespoon sugar
½ teaspoon salt
1¼ cups milk
1 can (8½ ounces) no-salt-added cream-style corn
½ cup egg substitute
3 tablespoons vegetable oil

Lightly grease CROCK-POT® Slow Cooker. In skillet over medium heat, cook onion, bell pepper and garlic until tender. Transfer to CROCK-POT® Slow Cooker. Stir in kidney beans and pinto beans. Add diced tomatoes and juice, tomato sauce, chili powder, black pepper, mustard and hot sauce. Cover and cook on High for 1 hour.

In mixing bowl, combine cornmeal, flour, baking powder, sugar and salt. Stir in milk, corn, egg substitute and vegetable oil. Spoon evenly over bean mixture. (There may be leftover cornbread depending on size of CROCK-POT® Slow Cooker being used; if there's remaining cornbread, spoon into greased muffin tins and bake at 375°F 30 minutes or until golden brown). Cover and cook on High 1½ to 2 more hours. Serve.

Makes 6 to 8 servings

Bean and Cornbread Casserole

BEAN POTPOURRI

2 cans (15 ounces each) garbanzo
   beans
1 can (16 ounces) pinto beans,
   undrained
1 pound cross-cut beef shank
½ pound smoked ham hock
4 medium potatoes, peeled and
   diced
3 to 4 ounces Polish sausage or
   knockwurst, thinly sliced
2½ cups water
1 large onion, thinly sliced
3 slices bacon, cooked and
   crumbled
1 teaspoon salt

Combine all ingredients in CROCK-POT® Slow Cooker; stir well. Cover and cook on Low 8 to 16 hours or on High 4 to 6 hours.

Makes 8 to 10 servings

MEATLESS SLOPPY JOES

2 cups thinly sliced onions
2 cups chopped green bell
    peppers
1 can (about 15 ounces) kidney
    beans, drained and mashed
1 can (8 ounces) tomato sauce
2 tablespoons ketchup
1 tablespoon prepared mustard
2 cloves garlic, finely chopped
1 teaspoon chili powder
    Cider vinegar (optional)
2 sandwich rolls, halved

Combine all ingredients except rolls in slow cooker. Cover and cook on Low 5 to 5½ hours or until vegetables are tender. Serve on rolls.

Makes 4 servings

BEAN AND VEGETABLE BURRITOS

2 tablespoons chili powder

2 teaspoons dried oregano leaves

1½ teaspoons ground cumin

1 large sweet potato, peeled and diced

1 can (15 ounces) black beans or pinto beans, drained and rinsed

4 cloves garlic, minced

1 medium onion, halved and thinly sliced

1 jalapeño pepper, seeded and minced*

1 green bell pepper, chopped

1 cup frozen corn, thawed and drained

3 tablespoons lime juice

1 tablespoon chopped cilantro

¾ cup (3 ounces) shredded Monterey Jack cheese

4 (10-inch) flour tortillas

Sour cream (optional)

Jalapeño peppers can sting and irritate the skin; wear rubber gloves when handling peppers and do not touch eyes. Wash hands after handling.

Combine chili powder, oregano and cumin in small bowl. Set aside.

Layer ingredients in slow cooker in the following order: sweet potato, beans, half of chili powder mix, garlic, onion, jalapeño pepper, bell pepper, remaining half of chili powder mix and corn. Cover and cook on Low 5 hours or until sweet potato is tender. Stir in lime juice and cilantro.

Preheat oven to 350°F. Spoon 2 tablespoons cheese in center of each tortilla. Top with 1 cup filling. Fold all 4 sides to enclose filling. Place burritos seam side down on baking sheet. Cover with foil and bake 20 to 30 minutes or until heated through. Serve with sour cream, if desired. *Makes 4 servings*

Bean and Vegetable Burrito

ARROZ CON QUESO

1 can (16 ounces) whole
    tomatoes, mashed
1 can (16 ounces) Mexican-style
    beans
1½ cups uncooked long-grain
    converted rice
2 cups (4 ounces) grated
    Monterey Jack or processed
    cheese, divided
1 large onion, finely chopped
1 cup cottage cheese
1 can (4 ounces) green chili
    peppers, drained, seeded and
    chopped
2 tablespoons vegetable oil
3 cloves garlic, minced

Mix all ingredients thoroughly except 1 cup grated cheese. Pour mixture into well-greased CROCK-POT® Slow Cooker. Cover and cook on Low 6 to 9 hours.

Just before serving, sprinkle with reserved 1 cup cheese.

Makes 6 to 8 servings

Arroz con Queso

BROCCOLI AND BEEF PASTA

2 cups broccoli florets *or*
    1 package (10 ounces) frozen broccoli, thawed
1 medium onion, thinly sliced
½ teaspoon dried basil leaves
½ teaspoon dried oregano leaves
½ teaspoon dried thyme leaves
1 can (14 ½ ounces) Italian-style diced tomatoes, undrained
¾ cup beef broth
1 pound lean ground beef
2 cloves garlic, minced
2 tablespoons tomato paste
2 cups cooked rotini pasta
3 ounces shredded Cheddar cheese or grated Parmesan cheese

Layer broccoli, onion, basil, oregano, thyme, tomatoes and beef broth in slow cooker. Cover and cook on Low for 2½ hours.

Combine beef and garlic in large nonstick skillet; cook over high heat 6 to 8 minutes or until meat is no longer pink, breaking meat apart with wooden spoon. Pour off drippings. Add beef mixture to slow cooker. Cover and cook 2 hours.

Stir in tomato paste. Add pasta and cheese. Cover and cook 30 minutes or until cheese melts and mixture is heated through.

Makes 4 servings

SERVING SUGGESTION: Serve with garlic bread.

Broccoli and Beef Pasta

MAIN DISHES

MACARONI AND CHEESE

3 cups cooked macaroni
1 tablespoon butter or margarine,
    melted
3 cups shredded sharp processed
    cheese
2 cups evaporated milk
¼ cup finely chopped green bell
    pepper
¼ cup chopped onion
1 teaspoon salt
¼ teaspoon black pepper

Toss macaroni with butter in large bowl. Add remaining ingredients. Pour into lightly greased CROCK-POT® Slow Cooker. Cover and cook on High 2 to 3 hours, stirring once or twice.

Makes 4 servings

SPAGHETTI MEAT SAUCE

½ **pound sweet or hot Italian link sausage**

1 **pound ground chuck**

1 **pound round steak or stewing beef, cut into 1-inch cubes**

2 **cans (16 ounces each) Italian-style tomatoes, broken up**

2 **medium onions, chopped**

1 **can (8 ounces) tomato sauce**

1 **can (6 ounces) tomato paste**

1 **large green bell pepper, seeded and chopped**

2 **tablespoons sugar**

1 **tablespoon salt**

2 **cloves garlic, minced**

2 **teaspoons dried basil leaves**

⅛ **teaspoon red pepper flakes**

Remove sausage from casing; brown in skillet with ground chuck and round steak. Break up sausage and ground meat with wooden spoon or fork as they brown; drain well. Add to CROCK-POT® Slow Cooker with remaining ingredients; stir well. Cover and cook on Low 8 to 16 hours or on High 4 to 6 hours. For thicker sauce, cook on High last 2 hours, removing cover for last hour. *Makes 12 to 16 servings*

NOTE: This sauce may be made 1 to 2 days in advance and refrigerated. It also freezes well.

MAIN DISHES

CHICKEN–MUSHROOM PASTA SAUCE

1 (2- to 3-pound) chicken, whole or cut up
2 onions, chopped
2 stalks celery, sliced
1 teaspoon salt
1 can (6 ounces) tomato paste
½ cup chicken broth or water
1 pound mushrooms, sliced
¼ cup dry sherry
1 teaspoon dried oregano leaves
2 tablespoons butter
2 tablespoons all-purpose flour
½ cup heavy cream or half-and-half

Place chicken in CROCK-POT® Slow Cooker with onions, celery and salt. Combine tomato paste with chicken broth and pour over ingredients in CROCK-POT® Slow Cooker. Add mushrooms, sherry and oregano; stir to moisten all ingredients. Cover and cook on Low 8 to 10 hours or on High 3½ to 5 hours.

Remove chicken; bone meat and dice. Return meat to CROCK-POT® Slow Cooker. Knead butter and flour together and add with cream; stir well. Cover and cook on Low 3 to 5 hours or on High 30 minutes to 1½ hours. *Makes 4 to 6 servings*

FRESH TOMATO SAUCE

4 cups peeled, seeded and finely chopped tomatoes
1 medium onion, minced
1 can (6 ounces) tomato paste
1½ teaspoons dried basil leaves
1 teaspoon sugar
3 cloves garlic, crushed

Combine all ingredients in lightly oiled CROCK-POT® Slow Cooker. Cover and cook on Low 6 to 12 hours or on High 4 hours. If thicker sauce is desired, remove cover and cook on High until sauce is reduced. *Makes about 5 cups*

TIP: This is good used in any recipe calling for tomato sauce.

NOTE: Double recipe for 5-quart CROCK-POT® Slow Cooker.

LASAGNA WITH WHITE SAUCE

1 package (8 ounces) mini lasagna noodles
1 pound ground beef
1 onion, chopped
1 can (14½ ounces) diced tomatoes
2 tablespoons tomato paste
1 beef bouillon cube
1½ teaspoons Italian seasoning
1 teaspoon salt
½ teaspoon black pepper
¼ teaspoon cayenne pepper

WHITE SAUCE

2 cups milk
2 cups shredded mozzarella cheese, divided
3 tablespoons all-purpose flour
2 tablespoons margarine or butter, melted
1 teaspoon salt
¼ teaspoon black pepper

Cook lasagna noodles in boiling water 5 minutes. Drain. In skillet, brown ground beef and onion until onion is tender. Drain fat. Transfer meat mixture to CROCK-POT® Slow Cooker. Stir in tomatoes, tomato paste, bouillon and seasonings. Add cooked lasagna noodles. To make white sauce, mix milk, 1 cup cheese, flour, margarine, salt and pepper in small bowl. Stir into CROCK-POT® Slow Cooker. Cover and cook on Low 4 to 6 hours or on High 2 to 3 hours. In last 30 minutes, turn CROCK-POT® Slow Cooker to High, if cooking on Low. Top with remaining mozzarella cheese. Serve when cheese is melted. *Makes 10 to 12 servings*

SPAGHETTI WITH MEATBALLS

1 can (28 ounces) Italian-style
     tomatoes, mashed
1 can (6 ounces) tomato paste
1 medium onion, finely chopped
2 tablespoons olive oil or butter
2 teaspoons salt
1 clove garlic, minced
1 teaspoon dried basil leaves
1 teaspoon dried oregano leaves
½ teaspoon sugar
¼ teaspoon red pepper flakes
     Meatballs (recipe follows,
         optional)
2 packages (16 ounces each)
     spaghetti
     Grated Parmesan cheese

Combine all ingredients except Meatballs, spaghetti and cheese in CROCK-POT® Slow Cooker; stir well. Cover and cook on Low 5 to 10 hours. Add Meatballs, if desired, and continue to cook on Low 7 to 12 hours.

Just before serving, cook spaghetti according to package directions. Serve topped with Meatballs in sauce and pass grated Parmesan cheese.   *Makes 10 to 12 servings*

MEATBALLS

1 pound lean ground beef
½ pound lean ground pork
¾ cup dry bread crumbs
⅓ cup pine nuts (optional)
2 eggs
¼ cup grated Parmesan cheese
¼ cup evaporated milk
2 tablespoons dried parsley flakes
1 teaspoon garlic salt
½ teaspoon dried basil leaves
½ teaspoon dried oregano leaves
¼ teaspoon dried thyme leaves
⅛ teaspoon freshly ground black pepper

Mix all ingredients thoroughly. Shape into 24 meatballs about 1½ inches in diameter. Place on baking sheet and bake in 450°F oven for 15 to 20 minutes or brown meatballs in skillet; drain.

RAVIOLI CASSEROLE

1½ pounds ground beef
1 medium onion, chopped
1 clove garlic, minced *or*
    ⅛ teaspoon garlic powder
2 cans (8 ounces each) tomato
    sauce
1 can (14 ounces) stewed
    tomatoes, undrained
1 teaspoon dried oregano leaves
1 teaspoon Italian seasoning
    Salt and black pepper to taste
1 package (16 ounces) bow-tie
    pasta, cooked
1 package (10 ounces) frozen
    chopped spinach, thawed
1½ cups shredded mozzarella
    cheese
½ cup grated Parmesan cheese

In large skillet over medium-high heat, brown ground beef, onion and garlic. Cook until onion is clear and soft, approximately 20 minutes. Drain excess fat. Transfer meat mixture to CROCK-POT® Slow Cooker.

Add tomato sauce, tomatoes, oregano, Italian seasoning, salt and pepper, stirring to break up stewed tomatoes. Cover and cook on Low 7 to 8 hours or on High 3½ to 4 hours. During last 30 minutes turn to High if on Low. Stir in cooked pasta, spinach and cheeses. Serve immediately when mozzarella cheese is melted.

Makes 6 servings

FUSILLI PIZZAIOLA WITH TURKEY MEATBALLS

2 cans (14½ ounces each) no-salt-added tomatoes, undrained
1 can (8 ounces) no-salt-added tomato sauce
¼ cup chopped onion
¼ cup grated carrot
2 tablespoons no-salt-added tomato paste
2 tablespoons chopped fresh basil
1 clove garlic, minced
½ teaspoon dried thyme leaves
¼ teaspoon sugar
¼ teaspoon black pepper, divided
1 bay leaf
1 pound ground turkey breast
1 egg, lightly beaten
1 tablespoon skim milk
¼ cup Italian-seasoned dry bread crumbs
2 tablespoons chopped fresh parsley
8 ounces uncooked fusilli or other spiral-shaped pasta

Combine tomatoes, tomato sauce, onion, carrot, tomato paste, basil, garlic, thyme, sugar, ⅛ teaspoon black pepper and bay leaf in slow cooker. Break up tomatoes gently with wooden spoon. Cover and cook on Low 4½ to 5 hours.

About 45 minutes before end of cooking, prepare meatballs. Preheat oven to 350°F. Combine turkey, egg and milk; blend in bread crumbs, parsley and remaining ⅛ teaspoon black pepper. With wet hands, shape mixture into small balls. Spray baking sheet with nonstick cooking spray. Arrange meatballs on baking sheet. Bake 25 minutes or until no longer pink in center.

Add meatballs to slow cooker. Cover and cook 45 minutes to 1 hour or until meatballs are heated through. Discard bay leaf. Prepare pasta according to package directions. Drain. Place in serving bowl; top with meatballs and sauce.

Makes 4 servings

Fusilli Pizzaiola with Turkey Meatballs

TUSCAN PASTA

**2 cans (14½ ounces each)
Italian-style stewed tomatoes,
undrained**

**1 pound boneless skinless
chicken breasts, cut into
1-inch pieces**

**1 can (15½ ounces) red kidney
beans, rinsed and drained**

1 can (15 ounces) tomato sauce

1 cup water

**1 medium green bell pepper,
chopped**

**1 jar (4½ ounces) sliced
mushrooms, drained**

½ cup chopped onion

½ cup chopped celery

4 cloves garlic, minced

1 teaspoon dried Italian seasoning

**6 ounces uncooked thin spaghetti,
broken into halves**

Place all ingredients except spaghetti in slow cooker. Cover and cook on Low 4 hours or until vegetables are tender.

Turn to High. Stir in spaghetti; cover. Stir again after 10 minutes. Cover and cook 45 minutes or until pasta is tender. Garnish with basil and bell pepper strips, if desired. *Makes 8 servings*

Tuscan Pasta

VEGGIE MAC AND TUNA

1½ cups (6 ounces) elbow macaroni
3 tablespoons butter or margarine
1 small onion, chopped
½ medium red bell pepper, chopped
½ medium green bell pepper, chopped
¼ cup all-purpose flour
1¾ cups milk
8 ounces cubed light pasteurized process cheese product
½ teaspoon dried marjoram leaves
1 package (10 ounces) frozen peas
1 can (9 ounces) tuna in water, drained

Cook macaroni according to package directions until just tender; drain. Melt butter in medium saucepan over medium heat. Add onion and bell peppers. Cook and stir 5 minutes or until tender. Add flour. Stir constantly over medium heat 2 minutes. Stir in milk and bring to a boil. Boil, stirring constantly, until thickened. Reduce heat to low; add cheese and marjoram. Stir until cheese is melted.

Combine macaroni, cheese sauce, peas and tuna in slow cooker. Cover and cook on Low 2½ hours or until bubbly at edge.

Makes 6 servings

Veggie Mac and Tuna

MONTEREY SPAGHETTI

4 ounces spaghetti, broken into 2-inch pieces

1 egg

1 cup sour cream

¼ cup grated Parmesan cheese

¼ teaspoon garlic powder

3 cups shredded Monterey Jack cheese, divided

1 package (10 ounces) frozen chopped spinach, thawed and drained

1 can (2.8 ounces) french fried onions, divided

Grease CROCK-POT® Slow Cooker. Cook spaghetti in boiling water 5 to 7 minutes. Drain. In small bowl, beat egg. Transfer to CROCK-POT® Slow Cooker. Add sour cream, Parmesan cheese and garlic powder. Mix spaghetti, 2 cups Monterey Jack cheese, spinach and half of onions in CROCK-POT® Slow Cooker. Cover and cook on Low 6 to 8 hours or on High 3 to 4 hours.

In last 30 minutes of cooking turn to High if cooking on Low and add remaining Monterey Jack cheese and onions to top of casserole. Serve when cheese is melted. *Makes 6 to 8 servings*

TURKEY AND TOMATO PASTA

1 can (28 ounces) whole tomatoes, chopped, undrained
1 can (14 ounces) whole tomatoes, chopped, undrained
1 cup cubed cooked turkey
2 teaspoons chili powder
1/2 teaspoon garlic powder
1 package (8 ounces) uncooked spiral pasta

Mix together tomatoes, turkey, chili powder and garlic powder in CROCK-POT® Slow Cooker. Turn on High and let mixture heat through, approximately 1 to 1½ hours. Once mixture is heated, stir in uncooked pasta. Cook an additional 30 minutes to 1 hour until pasta is tender. *Makes 4 (1-cup) servings*

MARINARA SAUCE

2 cans (28 ounces each) whole tomatoes
1 onion, finely chopped
2 carrots, peeled and finely chopped
1 clove garlic, chopped
2 tablespoons vegetable oil
1½ teaspoons sugar
1½ teaspoons salt

Place tomatoes in batches in blender container; blend until smooth (or purée tomatoes through food mill).

In skillet, sauté onion, carrots and garlic in oil just until tender (do not brown). Combine all ingredients in CROCK-POT® Slow Cooker; stir well. Cover and cook on Low 6 to 10 hours. Remove cover, stir well and cook on High last hour for thicker marinara sauce. *Makes about 6 cups*

MACARONI AND BEEF

1½ pounds lean ground beef
2 cups uncooked macaroni
2 cans (10¾ ounces each)
   condensed tomato soup
1 can (16 ounces) whole-kernel
   corn, drained
½ medium onion, chopped
1 can (4 ounces) sliced
   mushrooms, drained
Salt and black pepper

In skillet, brown ground beef; drain well. Put into CROCK-POT® Slow Cooker. Cook macaroni according to package directions until barely tender; drain well. Add macaroni and remaining ingredients to CROCK-POT® Slow Cooker. Stir just enough to blend. Cover and cook on Low 7 to 9 hours or on High 3 to 4 hours.

Makes 4 to 6 servings

Macaroni and Beef

MAIN DISHES

BREAKFAST CASSEROLE

1 pound ground turkey sausage
4 tablespoons chopped green
    onions
2 tablespoons vegetable oil
6 cups cubed French bread
2 cups (8 ounces) shredded
    reduced-fat mild Cheddar
    cheese
$2\frac{2}{3}$ cups skim milk
$1\frac{1}{4}$ cups frozen egg substitute,
    thawed
2 teaspoons prepared mustard
$\frac{1}{2}$ teaspoon ground black pepper

In skillet large, brown turkey sausage and green onions in vegetable oil. Drain meat. Coat 4-quart CROCK-POT® Slow Cooker with cooking spray and place bread cubes in bottom. Layer sausage mixture and cheese over bread. Combine milk, egg substitute, prepared mustard and pepper. Pour over sausage and cheese. Cover and cook on High 3 to 4 hours.

Makes 4 to 6 servings

CHEESY CHICKEN QUICHE

2 tablespoons corn oil
2 pounds boneless skinless
    chicken breasts, cut into cubes
¾ cup all-purpose flour
¾ teaspoon baking powder
½ teaspoon salt
1 cup evaporated milk
2 eggs, beaten
1 cup shredded Cheddar cheese
2 tablespoons chopped onion
2 teaspoons dried parsley flakes

Coat CROCK-POT® Slow Cooker with corn oil. Cook chicken on Low 6 to 8 hours or on High 3 to 4 hours or until fork tender. Stir together flour, baking powder, salt, milk and eggs. Fold in cheese, onion and parsley. Pour mixture over chicken and cook 1 hour on High. *Makes about 6 servings*

VARIATION: Cook 1 package (10 ounces) frozen chopped and thawed broccoli with chicken. Then pour in cheese, flour and egg mixture.

Slow Cooker

SIDE DISHES

ORANGE–SPICE GLAZED CARROTS

 1 package (32 ounces) baby carrots
 $\frac{1}{2}$ cup packed brown sugar
 $\frac{1}{2}$ cup orange juice
 3 tablespoons butter or margarine
 $\frac{3}{4}$ teaspoon ground cinnamon
 $\frac{1}{4}$ teaspoon ground nutmeg
 2 tablespoons cornstarch
 $\frac{1}{4}$ cup water

Combine all ingredients except cornstarch and water in slow cooker. Cover and cook on Low $3\frac{1}{2}$ to 4 hours or until carrots are crisp-tender. Spoon carrots into serving bowl. Remove juices to small saucepan. Heat to a boil. Mix cornstarch and water in small bowl until blended. Stir into saucepan. Boil 1 minute or until thickened; stir constantly. Pour over carrots.

Makes 6 servings

ASPARAGUS CASSEROLE

2 packages (10 ounces each) frozen asparagus spears, thawed

2 cups crushed saltine crackers

1 can (10¾ ounces) condensed cream of celery soup

1 can (10¾ ounces) condensed cream of chicken soup

1 cup cubed processed American cheese

½ cup slivered almonds

1 egg

In large bowl, combine all ingredients; stir well. Pour into lightly greased CROCK-POT® Slow Cooker. Cover and cook on High 3 to 3½ hours.

After cooking, dish may be held on Low up to 2 hours before serving.

Makes 4 to 6 servings

NOTE: 2 cans (14½ ounces each) asparagus pieces, drained, may be substituted for frozen asparagus.

Asparagus Casserole

CORN PUDDING

1 package (8 ounces) cream
cheese, softened
2 eggs, beaten
$\frac{1}{3}$ cup sugar
$2\frac{1}{3}$ cups fresh or frozen sweet corn
1 can (16 ounces) cream-style corn
1 package ($8\frac{1}{2}$ ounces) corn
bread muffin mix
1 cup milk
2 tablespoons margarine or
butter, melted
1 teaspoon salt
$\frac{1}{4}$ teaspoon ground nutmeg

Lightly grease CROCK-POT® Slow Cooker. In mixing bowl, blend cream cheese, eggs and sugar. Add remaining ingredients and mix well. Transfer to CROCK-POT® Slow Cooker. Cover and cook on High 3 to 4 hours. Serve. *Makes 10 to 12 servings*

SIDE DISHES

SWEET–AND–SOUR GREEN BEANS

2 packages (10 ounces each) frozen French-style green beans, partially thawed
4 slices bacon, diced
1 small onion, diced
1 tablespoon all-purpose flour
$\frac{1}{4}$ cup water
$\frac{1}{4}$ cup cider vinegar
2 tablespoons sugar
1 tablespoon chopped pimientos
$\frac{1}{2}$ teaspoon salt
Dash black pepper

Break apart green beans and place in CROCK-POT® Slow Cooker. In skillet, fry bacon until crisp; remove bacon to absorbent towels to drain. Pour off all but 2 tablespoons bacon drippings from skillet; sauté onion in bacon drippings (do not brown). Stir flour into water; stir into bacon drippings and cook until slightly thickened. Combine bacon and remaining ingredients; stir into thickened onion mixture. Pour over green beans and stir well. Cover and cook on High 1 hour, then turn to Low 7 to 9 hours.

Makes 6 to 8 servings

EGGPLANT ITALIANO

1¼ **pounds eggplant, cut into 1-inch cubes**
1 **can (16 ounces) diced tomatoes, undrained**
2 **medium onions, thinly sliced**
2 **ribs celery, cut into 1-inch pieces**
3 **tablespoons tomato sauce**
1 **tablespoon olive oil, divided**
½ **cup pitted black olives, cut in half**
2 **tablespoons balsamic vinegar**
1 **tablespoon sugar**
1 **tablespoon capers, drained**
1 **teaspoon dried oregano or basil leaves**
Salt and black pepper to taste
Fresh basil leaves, leaf lettuce and red jalapeño pepper for garnish

Combine eggplant, tomatoes, onions, celery, tomato sauce and oil in slow cooker. Cover and cook on Low 3½ to 4 hours or until eggplant is tender.

Stir in olives, vinegar, sugar, capers and oregano. Season with salt and pepper to taste. Cover and cook 45 minutes to 1 hour or until heated through. Garnish, if desired.   *Makes 6 servings*

Eggplant Italiano

SIDE DISHES

CARROTS LYONNAISE

1 chicken bouillon cube
1 cup boiling water
2 onions, sliced
¼ cup butter or margarine
1 tablespoon all-purpose flour
¼ teaspoon salt
6 carrots, peeled and cut into
    julienne strips
1 to 2 tablespoons sugar (optional)

Dissolve bouillon cube in boiling water; set aside. In large skillet, sauté onions in butter, stirring to separate rings and prevent browning. Stir flour and salt into slightly cooled bouillon; add to onions and cook until thickened. Combine carrots and onion sauce in CROCK-POT® Slow Cooker, stirring to coat carrots. Cover and cook on High 1 hour; turn to Low 2 to 6 hours. Before serving, add sugar to taste, if desired.

Makes 6 to 8 servings

SPOON BREAD, GEORGIA STYLE

1 can (17 ounces) cream-style corn
1 cup yellow cornmeal
1 cup grated sharp cheese
1 cup buttermilk
2 eggs
1 to 2 green chili peppers, seeded and diced
2 tablespoons vegetable oil or butter
2 teaspoons baking powder

Mix all ingredients well. Pour into greased and floured Bread 'n Cake Bake Pan; cover. Place in CROCK-POT® Slow Cooker. Cover and bake on High 2 to 3½ hours. *Do not unmold.* Serve warm, directly from the pan.

Makes 4 to 6 servings

SIDE DISHES

CORNMEAL MUSH

2 to 4 tablespoons butter or margarine, melted, divided
¼ teaspoon paprika
Dash cayenne pepper
6 cups boiling water
2 cups cornmeal (preferably water ground)
1 teaspoon salt

Use 1 tablespoon butter to lightly grease walls of CROCK-POT® Slow Cooker. Add paprika and cayenne pepper. Turn to High. Add water, cornmeal, salt and remaining butter to CROCK-POT® Slow Cooker; stir well. Cover and cook on Low 6 to 9 hours or on High 2 to 3 hours, stirring occasionally.

Makes 8 to 10 servings

FRIED CORNMEAL MUSH: Pour hot cornmeal into 2 lightly greased loaf pans. Chill overnight. To serve, cut into ¾-inch slices and fry in butter until browned.

HARVARD BEETS

½ cup sugar
2 tablespoons all-purpose flour
¼ cup water
¼ cup white vinegar
2 cans (16 ounces each) whole
  beets, drained

Mix sugar and flour; stir in water and vinegar. Place beets in CROCK-POT® Slow Cooker. Pour sugar-vinegar mixture over beets and stir to coat well. Cover and cook on High 3 to 4 hours.

Makes 4 to 6 servings

GREEN BEANS WITH SAVORY MUSHROOM SAUCE

2 packages (10 ounces each)
   frozen French-style green
   beans, thawed
1 can (10¾ ounces) condensed
   cream of mushroom soup
4 ounces (1½ cups) fresh
   mushrooms, sliced
¼ cup dry vermouth or dry white
   wine
½ teaspoon salt
½ teaspoon dried thyme leaves
¼ teaspoon black pepper
1 cup crushed prepared croutons
   or canned fried onion rings

Combine all ingredients except croutons in slow cooker. Mix until well blended. Cover and cook on Low 3 to 4 hours or until beans are crisp-tender. Sprinkle with croutons. Serve warm.

Makes 6 to 8 servings

Green Beans with Savory Mushroom Sauce

CREAMED CORN

2 packages (16 ounces each)
  frozen corn
2 packages (8 ounces each) cream
  cheese, softened and cubed
1 medium onion, chopped
  Black pepper to taste
  Garlic powder to taste

In CROCK-POT® Slow Cooker, combine corn, cream cheese, onion, pepper and garlic powder. Cover; cook on High 2 to 3 hours. *Makes 10 servings*

GOLDEN CAULIFLOWER

2 packages (10 ounces each)
  frozen cauliflower, thawed
  Salt and black pepper
1 can (11 ounces) condensed
  Cheddar cheese soup
4 slices bacon, fried and
  crumbled

Place cauliflower in CROCK-POT® Slow Cooker. Season with salt and pepper. Spoon soup over top; sprinkle with bacon. Cover and cook on High 1½ hours or on Low 4 to 5 hours. *Makes 4 to 6 servings*

GOLDEN BROCCOLI: Substitute frozen broccoli for frozen cauliflower.

SQUASH CASSEROLE

2 pounds yellow summer squash
    or zucchini, thinly sliced
    (about 6 cups)
1 can (10¾ ounces) condensed
    cream of chicken soup
1 cup shredded peeled carrot
½ medium onion, chopped
1 cup sour cream
¼ cup all-purpose flour
1 package (8 ounces) seasoned
    stuffing crumbs
½ cup butter or margarine, melted

In large bowl, combine squash, soup, carrot and onion. Mix sour cream and flour; stir into vegetables. Toss stuffing crumbs with butter and place half in CROCK-POT® Slow Cooker. Add vegetable mixture and top with remaining stuffing crumbs. Cover and cook on Low 6 to 8 hours.   *Makes 4 to 6 servings*

LOUISE'S BROCCOLI CASSEROLE

2 packages (10 ounces each) frozen broccoli spears, thawed and cut up
1 can (10¾ ounces) condensed cream of celery soup
1¼ cups (5 ounces) grated sharp Cheddar cheese, divided
¼ cup minced green onions
1 cup crushed saltine crackers or potato chips

In large bowl, combine broccoli, soup, 1 cup cheese and onions. Pour into lightly greased CROCK-POT® Slow Cooker. Sprinkle top with crushed crackers, then with remaining ¼ cup cheese. Cover and cook on Low 5 to 6 hours or on High 2½ to 3 hours.

Makes 4 to 6 servings

NOTE: If desired, casserole may be spooned into a baking dish and garnished with additional grated cheese and broken potato chips; bake 5 to 10 minutes in preheated 400°F oven.

Louise's Broccoli Casserole

ESCALLOPED CORN

  2 tablespoons butter or margarine
½ cup chopped onion
  3 tablespoons all-purpose flour
  1 cup milk
  4 cups frozen corn, thawed,
     divided
½ teaspoon salt
½ teaspoon dried thyme leaves
¼ teaspoon black pepper
⅛ teaspoon ground nutmeg
   Fresh thyme (optional)

Heat butter in small saucepan over medium heat. Add onion; cook and stir 5 minutes or until tender. Add flour. Cook over medium heat 1 minute, stirring constantly. Stir in milk and heat to a boil. Boil 1 minute or until thickened, stirring constantly.

Process half of corn in food processor or blender until coarsely chopped. Combine milk mixture, processed and whole corn, salt, dried thyme, pepper and nutmeg in slow cooker. Cover and cook on Low 3½ to 4 hours or until mixture is bubbly around edge. Garnish with fresh thyme, if desired. *Makes 6 servings*

VARIATION: If desired, add ½ cup (2 ounces) shredded Cheddar cheese and 2 tablespoons grated Parmesan cheese before serving; stir until melted. Garnish with additional shredded Cheddar cheese, if desired.

Escalloped Corn

SUNSHINE SQUASH

1 butternut squash (about
    2 pounds) peeled, seeded
    and diced
1 can (about 15 ounces) whole
    kernel corn, drained
1 can (14½ ounces) tomatoes,
    undrained
1 medium onion, coarsely
    chopped
1 green bell pepper, seeded and
    cut into 1-inch pieces
½ cup chicken broth
1 canned green chili, coarsely
    chopped
1 clove garlic, minced
½ teaspoon salt
¼ teaspoon black pepper
1 tablespoon plus 1½ teaspoons
    tomato paste

Combine all ingredients except tomato paste in slow cooker. Cover and cook on Low 6 hours or until squash is tender.

Remove about ¼ cup cooking liquid and blend with tomato paste. Stir into slow cooker. Cook 30 minutes or until mixture is slightly thickened and heated through.	*Makes 6 to 8 servings*

SPINACH NOODLE CASSEROLE

1 package (8 ounces) spinach noodles

2 tablespoons vegetable oil or melted butter

1½ cups (12 ounces) sour cream

⅓ cup all-purpose flour

1½ cups small-curd cream-style cottage cheese

4 green onions with tops, finely minced

2 teaspoons garlic salt

2 teaspoons Worcestershire sauce
Dash hot pepper sauce

Cook noodles according to package directions until barely tender. Rinse in cold water and drain. Toss with oil. In large bowl, mix sour cream and flour. Stir in remaining ingredients. Add noodles and stir well to coat. Pour into well-greased CROCK-POT® Slow Cooker. Cover and cook on High 1½ to 2½ hours. If desired, serve with additional sour cream. *Makes 8 servings*

HUNGARIAN NOODLE SIDE DISH

3 chicken bouillon cubes

¼ cup boiling water

1 can (10¾ ounces) cream of mushroom soup

½ cup chopped onion

2 tablespoons Worcestershire sauce

1 tablespoon poppy seeds

¼ teaspoon garlic powder

¼ teaspoon hot pepper sauce

2 cups cottage cheese

2 cups sour cream

1 package (16 ounces) wide egg noodles, cooked and drained

¼ cup shredded Parmesan cheese

Paprika

Lightly grease CROCK-POT® Slow Cooker. In large bowl, dissolve bouillon in water. Add soup, onion, Worcestershire sauce, poppy seeds, garlic powder and hot pepper sauces. Stir in cottage cheese, sour cream and noodles. Transfer to CROCK-POT® Slow Cooker. Sprinkle with Parmesan cheese and paprika. Cover and cook on High 3 to 4 hours. Serve immediately. *Makes 8 to 10 servings*

CHEESY TURKEY COTTAGE FRIES

- 3 to 4 cups frozen cottage-style potatoes
- 2 cups cubed cooked turkey
- 2 cups frozen cut broccoli, thawed and drained
- 1 cup pasteurized processed cheese product
- 1 jar (2 ounces) diced pimientos, drained

Spray inside of CROCK-POT® Slow Cooker with cooking spray. Place potatoes in layer in bottom of CROCK-POT® Slow Cooker. Stir remaining ingredients together and pour over potatoes. Cook on Low 6 to 8 hours or on High 3 to 4 hours.

Makes 4 (1-cup) servings

CHEESE POTATO PUFF

- 12 medium potatoes, peeled and quartered
- 1 teaspoon salt, divided
- 2 cups shredded Cheddar cheese
- 1 cup milk
- ¾ cup margarine or butter, melted
- 2 eggs, beaten
  Chopped dried chives for garnish

Lightly grease CROCK-POT® Slow Cooker. Place potatoes in large saucepan with ½ teaspoon salt; cover with water and boil until tender (15 minutes). Drain potatoes, then mash. Transfer to CROCK-POT® Slow Cooker. Stir in cheese, milk, margarine, eggs and remaining ½ teaspoon salt. Cover and cook on High 3 to 4 hours. Top with chives, if desired. Serve immediately.

Makes 10 to 12 servings

SWEET POTATO CASSEROLE

2 cans (18 ounces each) sweet
      potatoes, drained and mashed
$\frac{1}{3}$ cup plus 2 tablespoons
      margarine or butter, melted,
      divided
2 tablespoons granulated sugar
$\frac{1}{3}$ cup plus 2 tablespoons brown
      sugar, divided
2 eggs, beaten
$\frac{1}{2}$ cup milk
1 tablespoon orange juice
$\frac{1}{3}$ cup chopped pecans
2 tablespoons all-purpose flour

Lightly grease CROCK-POT® Slow Cooker. Mix sweet potatoes, $\frac{1}{3}$ cup margarine, granulated sugar and 2 tablespoons brown sugar in large bowl. Beat in eggs, milk and orange juice. Transfer to CROCK-POT® Slow Cooker.

Combine pecans, remaining $\frac{1}{3}$ cup brown sugar, flour and remaining 2 tablespoons margarine. Spread over sweet potatoes.

Cover and cook on High 3 to 4 hours. Serve.

Makes 6 to 8 servings

Sweet Potato Casserole

CREAM CHEESE POTATOES

2 tablespoons minced or chopped dried onion
2 cloves garlic, minced *or*
   ¼ teaspoon garlic powder
1 teaspoon salt
¼ teaspoon black pepper
8 medium potatoes, scrubbed and sliced (about 2 pounds)
1 package (8 ounces) cream cheese, cut into cubes

Lightly grease CROCK-POT® Slow Cooker. In small bowl, combine onion, garlic, salt and pepper. Layer ¼ of sliced potatoes in bottom of CROCK-POT® Slow Cooker. Sprinkle with ¼ of seasonings. Layer with ⅓ of cream cheese cubes. Continue layering process, ending with layer of potatoes then sprinkle with seasonings. Cover and cook on High 3 to 4 hours. In last hour of cooking, stir potatoes to distribute cream cheese. Serve when potatoes are tender. *Makes 4 to 6 servings*

NOTE: If desired, potatoes can be slightly mashed prior to serving.

TIP: Cook potatoes in boiling water for about 30 minutes or until tender and then cut into strips. Mixture should be cooked on Low 6 to 8 hours or on High about 2 hours, until potatoes are tender.

VARIATION: Substitute 2 packages (16 ounces each) frozen hashbrowns for potatoes and prepare as directed. Cook on Low 4 to 6 hours or on High 2 hours or until potatoes are tender.

SCALLOPED POTATOES

    1 package (16 ounces) frozen
        hash brown potatoes
1½ cups milk
    1 can (10¾ ounces) cream of
        mushroom soup
    1 cup (4 ounces) shredded
        Cheddar cheese
    1 small green bell pepper, cut into
        small pieces
  ½ cup margarine or butter, melted
  ¼ cup dried chopped onion
    2 tablespoons chopped pimientos
  ⅛ teaspoon black pepper
    1 cup cheese cracker crumbs,
        divided

Lightly grease CROCK-POT® Slow Cooker. Stir together potatoes, milk, soup, cheese, bell pepper, margarine, onion, pimientos, black pepper and ½ cup cracker crumbs. Transfer to CROCK-POT® Slow Cooker. Top with remaining cracker crumbs. Cover and cook on High 3 to 4 hours. Serve. *Makes 6 to 8 servings*

RUSTIC POTATOES AU GRATIN

½ cup milk
1 can (10¾ ounces) condensed
    Cheddar cheese soup
1 package (8 ounces) cream
    cheese, softened
1 clove garlic, minced
¼ teaspoon ground nutmeg
⅛ teaspoon black pepper
2 pounds baking potatoes, cut
    into ¼-inch slices
1 small onion, thinly sliced
    Paprika (optional)

Heat milk in small saucepan over medium heat until small bubbles form around edge of pan. Remove from heat. Add soup, cheese, garlic, nutmeg and pepper. Stir until smooth. Layer ¼ of potatoes and ¼ of onion in bottom of slow cooker. Top with ¼ of soup mixture. Repeat layers 3 times, using remaining potatoes, onion and soup mixture. Cover and cook on Low 6½ to 7 hours or until potatoes are tender and most of liquid is absorbed. Sprinkle with paprika, if desired. *Makes 6 servings*

Rustic Potatoes au Gratin

CHEESY POTATO CASSEROLE

**7 medium potatoes (about
  2 pounds)**
**1 can (10¾ ounces) cream of
  chicken soup**
1 container (8 ounces) sour cream
**1 small onion, chopped *or*
  1 tablespoon minced onion**
**¼ cup plus 3 tablespoons butter
  or margarine, melted, divided**
1 teaspoon salt
**2 cups (8 ounces) shredded
  Cheddar cheese**
**1½ to 2 cups herb-seasoning
  stuffing mix**

Peel potatoes and cut into ¼-inch strips; set aside.

Combine soup, sour cream, onion, ¼ cup butter and salt in bowl.

Lightly butter inside of 5-quart CROCK-POT® Slow Cooker and place potatoes inside. Mix cheese with potatoes. Pour soup mixture into CROCK-POT® Slow Cooker; mix well. Cover top of potato mixture with stuffing mix and drizzle with remaining 3 tablespoons butter. Cover; cook on Low 8 to 10 hours until potatoes are tender or on High 5 to 6 hours.

Makes 8 to 10 servings

TIP: Cook potatoes in boiling water about 30 minutes or until tender and then cut into strips. Mixture should be cooked on Low 6 to 8 hours or on High about 2 hours, until potatoes are tender.

VARIATION: Substitute 2 packages (16 ounces each) frozen hashbrowns for potatoes and prepare as directed. Cook on Low 4 to 6 hours or on High 2 hours.

Cheesy Potato Casserole

OUR BEST BAKED BEANS

2 cans (16 ounces each) baked
   beans, drained
½ green bell pepper, seeded and
   chopped
½ medium onion, chopped
½ cup packed brown sugar
½ cup ketchup
½ cup hickory-smoke barbecue
   sauce
5 slices bacon, fried and crumbled
1½ teaspoons prepared mustard

Mix all ingredients in CROCK-POT® Slow Cooker. Cover and cook on Low 8 to 12 hours or on High 3 to 4 hours.

Makes 6 to 8 servings

OLD-FASHIONED BAKED BEANS

1 pound dried navy beans
1 pound smoked ham, bacon or
    salt pork, diced
1 medium onion, finely chopped
½ cup packed brown sugar
½ cup ketchup
½ cup dark corn syrup
1 teaspoon paprika
½ teaspoon dried basil leaves
    Salt

Completely soften beans (see Note). Drain and combine beans with remaining ingredients in large bowl. Pour into CROCK-POT® Slow Cooker. Cover and cook on Low 6 to 12 hours or on High 3 to 4 hours.

Makes 8 servings

NOTE: Cooking with dried beans can be tricky, even in a CROCK-POT® Slow Cooker. The minerals in the water and variations in voltage affect different types of beans in different ways. For best results, keep these points in mind: Dried beans, especially red kidney beans, should be boiled before adding to a recipe. Cover the beans with 3 times their volume of unsalted water and bring to a boil. Boil 10 minutes and reduce heat. Beans must be softened completely before combining with sugar and/or acidic foods. (Note: sugar and acid have a hardening effect on beans and will prevent softening.) After boiling beans 10 minutes, reduce heat, cover and allow to simmer 1½ hours or until beans are tender. Soaking in water, if desired, should be completed before boiling. Discard water after soaking or boiling.

MRS. GRADY'S BEANS

½ pound lean ground beef
1 small onion, chopped
8 slices bacon, chopped
1 can (about 15 ounces) pinto
    beans, undrained
1 can (about 15 ounces) butter
    beans, rinsed and drained,
    reserve ¼ cup liquid
1 can (about 15 ounces) kidney
    beans, rinsed and drained
¼ cup ketchup
2 tablespoons molasses
½ teaspoon dry mustard
½ cup granulated sugar
¼ cup packed brown sugar

Brown ground beef, onion and bacon in medium saucepan over high heat. Stir in beans and liquid; set aside.

Combine ketchup, molasses and mustard in medium bowl. Mix in sugars. Stir ketchup mixture into beef mixture; mix well. Transfer to slow cooker. Cover and cook on Low 2 to 3 hours or until heated through. *Makes 6 to 8 servings*

LIMA BEAN CASEROLE

3 packages (10 ounces each) frozen baby lima beans, thawed
2 cans (10¾ ounces each) condensed cream of celery soup
2 small onions, thinly sliced
2 cans (4 ounces each) sliced mushrooms, undrained
1 jar (2 ounces) chopped pimientos, drained
2 teaspoons salt
⅛ teaspoon black pepper
½ teaspoon dill seed
½ cup heavy cream
1 cup grated Parmesan cheese

Combine all ingredients except cream and Parmesan cheese in CROCK-POT® Slow Cooker; stir well. Cover and cook on Low 10 to 12 hours. Add cream just before serving; stir well. Sprinkle Parmesan cheese on top. *Makes 8 to 10 servings*

BEAN POT MEDLEY

1 can (15½ ounces) black beans, rinsed and drained

1 can (15½ ounces) red beans, rinsed and drained

1 can (15½ ounces) Great Northern beans, rinsed and drained

1 can (15½ ounces) black-eyed peas, rinsed and drained

1½ cups ketchup

1 can (8½ ounces) baby lima beans, rinsed and drained

1 cup chopped onion

1 cup chopped red bell pepper

1 cup chopped green bell pepper

½ cup packed brown sugar

½ cup water

2 to 3 teaspoons cider vinegar

1 teaspoon dry mustard

2 bay leaves

⅛ teaspoon black pepper

Combine all ingredients in slow cooker; stir. Cover and cook on Low 6 to 7 hours or until onion and bell peppers are tender. Remove and discard bay leaves. *Makes 8 servings*

Bean Pot Medley

NEW ENGLAND BAKED BEANS

4 slices bacon, chopped
3 cans (15 ounces each) Great Northern beans, rinsed and drained
¾ cup water
1 small onion, chopped
⅓ cup canned diced tomatoes, well drained
3 tablespoons firmly packed brown sugar
3 tablespoons maple syrup
3 tablespoons unsulphured molasses
2 cloves garlic, minced
½ teaspoon salt
½ teaspoon dry mustard
⅛ teaspoon black pepper
½ bay leaf

Cook bacon in large skillet until almost cooked but not crispy. Drain on paper towels.

Combine bacon and all remaining ingredients in slow cooker. Cover and cook on Low 6 to 8 hours or until onions are tender and mixture is thickened. Remove and discard bay leaf before serving. *Makes 4 to 6 servings*

New England Baked Beans

SPICY WESTERN BEANS

$\frac{1}{3}$ cup lentils
1$\frac{1}{3}$ cups water
4 slices bacon, fried, diced and
    drippings reserved
1 onion, chopped
1 can (16 ounces) pinto beans,
    undrained
1 can (16 ounces) red kidney
    beans, undrained
1 can (14 ounces) whole tomatoes,
    undrained, chopped
2 tablespoons ketchup
1 teaspoon garlic powder
$\frac{3}{4}$ teaspoon chili powder
$\frac{1}{2}$ teaspoon ground cumin
$\frac{1}{4}$ teaspoon red pepper flakes
1 bay leaf

Boil lentils in water 20 to 30 minutes. Drain. In bacon drippings, cook onion until transparent. Combine lentils, beans, tomatoes, bacon, onion mixture, ketchup, garlic powder, chili powder, cumin, red pepper flakes and bay leaf in CROCK-POT® Slow Cooker. Cook on High 3 to 4 hours. Remove and discard bay leaf. Serve.

Makes 8 to 10 servings

Spicy Western Beans

BEAN CASSEROLE

3 cans (16 ounces each) pork and
  beans, drained
1 can (16 ounces) pork and
  beans, undrained
1 cup (4 ounces) shredded sharp
  Cheddar cheese
¾ cup chopped onion
4 tablespoons brown sugar
4 tablespoons Worcestershire
  sauce
2 tablespoons white vinegar
1 tablespoon plus 1 teaspoon chili
  powder
1 tablespoon prepared mustard
8 slices bacon, fried and
  crumbled

Lightly grease CROCK-POT® Slow Cooker. Combine beans, cheese, onion, brown sugar, Worcestershire sauce, vinegar, chili powder and mustard in CROCK-POT® Slow Cooker. Top with bacon. Cover and cook on Low 6 to 8 hours or on High 3 to 4 hours. Serve. *Makes 8 to 10 servings*

WILD RICE CASSEROLE

2½ cups water

2 medium onions, finely chopped

3 ribs celery, thinly sliced

2 packages (7 ounces each) wild rice and long-grain converted rice mix

1 can (10¾ ounces) condensed cream of mushroom soup

½ pound processed American cheese, cubed

½ cup butter or margarine, melted

1 can (4 ounces) sliced mushrooms, drained

Combine all ingredients in CROCK-POT® Slow Cooker; stir thoroughly. Cover and cook on Low 6 to 10 hours or on High 2 to 3½ hours.

Makes 6 to 8 servings

RISI BISI

1½ **cups uncooked converted**
     long-grain white rice
¾ **cup chopped onion**
2 **cloves garlic, minced**
2 **cans (about 14 ounces each)**
     reduced-sodium chicken broth
⅓ **cup water**
¾ **teaspoon Italian seasoning**
½ **teaspoon dried basil leaves**
½ **cup frozen peas, thawed**
¼ **cup grated Parmesan cheese**
¼ **cup toasted pine nuts (optional)**

Combine rice, onion and garlic in slow cooker. Heat broth and water in small saucepan to a boil. Stir boiling liquid, Italian seasoning and basil into rice mixture. Cover and cook on Low 2 to 3 hours or until liquid is absorbed. Add peas. Cover and cook 1 hour. Stir in cheese. Spoon rice into serving bowl. Sprinkle with pine nuts, if desired.   *Makes 6 servings*

Risi Bisi

GOLDEN CHEESE BAKE

3 cups grated peeled carrots
2 cups cooked long-grain
    converted rice
2 cups (8 ounces) grated sharp
    processed cheese
½ cup milk
2 eggs, beaten
2 tablespoons chopped onion
1 teaspoon salt
¼ teaspoon black pepper

In bowl, combine all ingredients; stir well. Pour into greased CROCK-POT® Slow Cooker. Cover and cook on Low 7 to 9 hours or on High 2½ to 3 hours. *Makes 4 to 6 servings*

NOTE: Double recipe for 5-quart CROCK-POT® Slow Cooker.

BROWN–AND–WHITE RICE

8 slices bacon, diced
½ cup uncooked brown rice
3 cups beef broth
1 cup uncooked long-grain converted rice
4 green onions with tops, sliced
1 can (4 ounces) sliced mushrooms, drained
⅓ cup slivered almonds, toasted
3 tablespoons grated Parmesan cheese

In skillet, fry bacon until partially crisp but still limp. Stir in brown rice and cook over medium heat until rice is light golden brown. Add bacon and browned rice to CROCK-POT® Slow Cooker with beef broth, converted rice, green onions and mushrooms; stir well. Cover and cook on Low 6 to 8 hours or on High 2½ to 3½ hours. Before serving, stir well and season with salt if needed. Garnish with almonds and cheese.

Makes 6 to 8 servings

SPICY RICE CASSEROLE

4 cups boiling water
4 beef bouillon cubes
2 pounds mild bulk pork sausage
2 teaspoons ground cumin
1 teaspoon garlic powder
4 medium onions, chopped
4 medium green bell peppers,
  chopped
2 packages (6¼ ounces each)
  converted long-grain and wild
  rice mix
3 jalapeño peppers, seeded and
  minced

Pour boiling water into CROCK-POT® Slow Cooker that has been set to High. Stir in bouillon cubes. Brown sausage, cumin and garlic powder in skillet. Drain. Add onions and bell peppers; sauté until tender, about 15 to 20 minutes. Transfer to CROCK-POT® Slow Cooker. Stir in rice and jalapeño peppers.

Cover and cook on High 1 hour, then turn to Low and cook 1 to 2 more hours. Serve. *Makes 10 to 12 servings*

NOTE: If a spicier rice casserole is desired, add seasoning mix that is included with rice.

Spicy Rice Casserole

PESTO RICE AND BEANS

    1 can (15 ounces) Great Northern
        beans, rinsed and drained
    1 can (14 ounces) chicken broth
    ¾ cup uncooked long-grain white
        rice
  1½ cups frozen cut green beans,
        thawed and drained
    ½ cup prepared pesto sauce
      Grated Parmesan cheese
      (optional)

Combine Great Northern beans, chicken broth and rice in slow cooker. Cover and cook on Low 2 hours.

Stir in green beans; cover and cook 1 hour or until rice and green beans are tender. Turn off slow cooker and remove insert to heatproof surface. Stir in pesto sauce and cheese, if desired. Let stand, covered, 5 minutes or until cheese has melted. Serve immediately. *Makes 8 servings*

RED RICE

5 slices bacon
1 large onion, chopped
2 cans (16 ounces each) chopped
    peeled tomatoes, undrained
1 cup uncooked converted
    long-grain rice
1 cup finely chopped cooked ham
$\frac{1}{2}$ teaspoon salt
$\frac{1}{4}$ teaspoon black pepper
$\frac{1}{8}$ teaspoon hot sauce

Fry bacon in skillet. Remove bacon and crumble. Cook onion in bacon drippings over medium-high heat until tender. Combine bacon, onion, tomatoes with juice, rice, ham and seasonings in CROCK-POT® Slow Cooker. Cover and cook on Low 6 to 8 hours or on High 3 to 4 hours. Serve. *Makes 6 to 8 servings*

NOTE: If hotter rice is desired, add more hot sauce to taste.

CRACKED WHEAT PILAF

  5 cups beef broth
  2 cups cracked wheat or bulgur
  1 medium onion, chopped
  ¼ cup butter, melted
  ¼ cup minced parsley *or*
       2 tablespoons dried parsley
       flakes
  Salt to taste

Combine all ingredients in CROCK-POT® Slow Cooker; stir well. Cover and cook on Low 10 to 12 hours or on High 3 to 4 hours, stirring occasionally.

Makes 6 to 8 servings

CHICKEN STUFFING

**1 package (12-serving size)
   chicken stuffing mix
3 cans (10¾ ounces each) cream
   of chicken soup, divided
3 to 4 cups cubed cooked chicken
½ cup milk
2 cups shredded mild Cheddar
   cheese**

Prepare stuffing mix according to package directions and place in 5-quart CROCK-POT® Slow Cooker. Stir in 2 cans soup. In mixing bowl, stir together cubed chicken, remaining 1 can soup and milk. Spread over stuffing in CROCK-POT® Slow Cooker. Sprinkle cheese over top. Cover and cook on Low 4 to 6 hours or on High 2 to 3 hours.   *Makes 8 to 10 servings*

Slow Cooker

BREADS & TREATS

BOSTON BROWN BREAD

3 (16-ounce) emptied and cleaned
   vegetable cans
½ cup rye flour
½ cup yellow cornmeal
½ cup whole wheat flour
3 tablespoons sugar
1 teaspoon baking soda
¾ teaspoon salt
½ cup chopped walnuts
½ cup raisins
1 cup buttermilk*
⅓ cup molasses

*Soured fresh milk may be substituted. To sour, place 1 tablespoon lemon juice plus enough milk to equal 1 cup in 2-cup measure. Stir; let stand 5 minutes before using.

Spray vegetable cans and 1 side of three 6-inch-square pieces of aluminum foil with nonstick cooking spray; set aside. Combine rye flour, cornmeal, whole wheat flour, sugar, baking soda and salt in large bowl. Stir in walnuts and raisins. Whisk buttermilk and molasses in medium bowl until blended. Add buttermilk mixture to dry ingredients; stir until well mixed. Spoon mixture evenly into prepared cans. Place 1 piece of foil, greased side down, on top of each can. Secure foil with rubber bands or cotton string.

Place filled cans in slow cooker. Pour boiling water into slow cooker to come halfway up sides of cans. (Make sure foil tops do not touch boiling water.) Cover and cook on Low 4 hours or until skewer inserted in centers comes out clean. To remove bread, lay cans on side; roll and tap gently on all sides until bread releases. Cool completely on wire racks. *Makes 3 loaves*

ORANGE DATE–NUT BREAD

1 cup snipped dates
4 teaspoons finely shredded
    orange peel
⅔ cup boiling water
⅓ cup orange juice
¾ cup sugar
2 tablespoons shortening
1 egg, slightly beaten
1 teaspoon vanilla
2 cups all-purpose flour
1 teaspoon baking powder
½ teaspoon baking soda
¼ teaspoon salt
½ cup chopped nuts, such as
    pecans or walnuts

Grease and flour inside of Bread 'n Cake Bake Pan.

In large bowl, combine snipped dates and orange peel. Stir in boiling water and orange juice. Add sugar, shortening, egg and vanilla, stirring just until mixed.

In medium bowl, combine flour, baking powder, baking soda and salt. Add flour mixture to date mixture. Stir in nuts. Pour into prepared Bread 'n Cake Bake Pan. Place cover on Bread 'n Cake Bake Pan.

Place Bread 'n Cake Bake Pan in CROCK-POT® Slow Cooker. Cover CROCK-POT® Slow Cooker and bake on High 1½ to 2 hours. Check bread after 1½ hours for doneness. Bread is done when sides start pulling away from pan. *Makes 1 loaf*

WHOLE WHEAT BANANA BREAD

⅔ cup margarine or butter
1 cup sugar
1 cup mashed bananas (2 to 3 bananas)
2 eggs
1 cup whole wheat flour
1 cup all-purpose flour
½ cup chopped pecans or walnuts
¼ cup wheat germ
1 teaspoon baking soda
½ teaspoon salt

Grease and flour inside of Bread 'n Cake Bake Pan.

Cream margarine with electric mixer. Blend in sugar. Add mashed bananas and eggs. Beat until smooth.

In small bowl, combine flours, pecans, wheat germ, baking soda and salt. Add to creamed mixture. Pour into prepared Bread 'n Cake Bake Pan. Place lid on pan. Put Bread 'n Cake Bake Pan in CROCK-POT® Slow Cooker. Cover CROCK-POT® Slow Cooker. Cook on High 3 to 4 hours. Check after 3 hours for doneness. Bread is done when it is pulling away from sides of Bread 'n Cake Bake Pan.

When bread is done remove Bread 'n Cake Bake Pan from CROCK-POT® Slow Cooker. Let bread cool then invert bread on plate and invert again for serving. *Makes 1 loaf*

HONEY WHEAT BREAD

3 cups whole wheat flour, divided

¾ to 1 cup all-purpose flour, divided

2 cups warm reconstituted dry milk*

¼ cup honey

2 tablespoons vegetable oil

1 package active dry yeast

¾ teaspoon salt

Fresh milk may be used if scalded.

Combine half of flours, warm (not hot) milk, honey, oil, yeast and salt. With electric mixer, beat well about 2 minutes. Add remaining flours; mix well. Place dough in well-greased Bread 'n Cake Bake Pan; cover. Let stand 5 minutes. Place pan in 3½- or 5-quart CROCK-POT® Slow Cooker. Cover and bake on High 2 to 3 hours.

Remove pan and uncover. Let stand 5 minutes. Unmold and serve warm.

Makes 1 loaf

WHITE BREAD

1 package active dry yeast
$\frac{1}{4}$ cup plus 1 teaspoon sugar, divided
$\frac{1}{4}$ cup warm water
$3\frac{1}{2}$ to 4 cups all-purpose flour, divided
1 cup lukewarm water
$\frac{1}{4}$ cup vegetable oil
1 egg
1 teaspoon salt

In large bowl, dissolve yeast and 1 teaspoon sugar in $\frac{1}{4}$ cup warm water. Allow to stand until it bubbles and foams. Add 2 cups flour, remaining $\frac{1}{4}$ cup sugar, lukewarm water, oil, egg and salt. Beat with electric mixer 2 minutes. With wooden spoon, stir in remaining $1\frac{1}{2}$ to 2 cups flour until dough leaves side of bowl. Place dough in well-greased Bread 'n Cake Bake Pan; cover. Place pan in $3\frac{1}{2}$- or 5-quart CROCK-POT® Slow Cooker. Cover and bake on High 2 to 3 hours or until edges are browned.

Remove pan and uncover. Let stand 5 minutes. Unmold on cake rack.

Makes 1 loaf

FRUIT & NUT BAKED APPLES

4 large baking apples, such as
    Rome Beauty or Jonathan
1 tablespoon lemon juice
$\frac{1}{3}$ cup chopped dried apricots
$\frac{1}{3}$ cup chopped walnuts or pecans
3 tablespoons packed brown sugar
$\frac{1}{2}$ teaspoon ground cinnamon
2 tablespoons melted butter or
    margarine

Scoop out center of each apple, leaving 1½-inch-wide cavity about ½ inch from bottom. Peel top of apple down about 1 inch. Brush peeled edges evenly with lemon juice. Mix apricots, walnuts, brown sugar and cinnamon in small bowl. Add butter; mix well. Spoon mixture evenly into apple cavities.

Pour ½ cup water in bottom of slow cooker. Place 2 apples in bottom of cooker. Arrange remaining 2 apples above but not directly on top of bottom apples. Cover and cook on Low 3 to 4 hours or until apples are tender. Serve warm or at room temperature with caramel ice cream topping, if desired.

Makes 4 servings

HINT: Ever wonder why you need to brush lemon juice around the top of an apple? Citrus fruits contain an acid that keeps apples, potatoes and other white vegetables from discoloring once they are cut or peeled.

Fruit & Nut Baked Apples

POACHED PEARS WITH RASPBERRY SAUCE

4 cups cran-raspberry juice
    cocktail
2 cups Rhine or Riesling wine
¼ cup sugar
2 cinnamon sticks, broken into
    halves
4 to 5 firm Bosc or Anjou pears,
    peeled, cored and seeded
1 package (10 ounces) frozen
    raspberries in syrup, thawed
Fresh berries (optional)

Combine juice, wine, sugar and cinnamon stick halves in slow cooker. Submerge pears in mixture. Cover and cook on Low 3½ to 4 hours or until pears are tender. Remove and discard cinnamon sticks.

Process raspberries in food processor or blender until smooth; strain out seeds. Spoon raspberry sauce onto serving plates; place pear on top of sauce. Garnish with fresh berries, if desired.

Makes 4 to 5 servings

Poached Pears with Raspberry Sauce

STEWED FRUIT AND DUMPLINGS

2 pints fresh or frozen fruit, such
    as strawberries, raspberries,
    blueberries or peaches
½ cup plus 2 tablespoons
    granulated sugar, divided
½ cup warm water
2 tablespoons quick-cooking
    tapioca
2 cups all-purpose flour
2½ teaspoons baking powder
½ teaspoon salt
5 tablespoons margarine or
    butter, cut in cubes
½ cup milk
1 egg
2 tablespoons brown sugar

In CROCK-POT® Slow Cooker, combine fruit, ½ cup granulated sugar, water and tapioca. Cover and cook on Low 5 to 6 hours or on High 2½ to 3 hours or until fruit has formed a thick sauce.

In mixing bowl, combine flour, remaining 2 tablespoons granulated sugar, baking powder and salt. Use pastry blender or 2 knives to cut in margarine until mixture resembles coarse meal. In small bowl, stir together milk and egg. Pour egg mixture into flour mixture and stir until soft dough is formed.

Turn CROCK-POT® Slow Cooker to High if it is on Low. Drop dough by teaspoonfuls on top of fruit. Cover and cook 30 minutes to 1 hour or until toothpick inserted into dumplings comes out clean. Sprinkle with brown sugar. Serve warm.

Makes 8 to 10 servings

PEACH COBBLER

¾ cup all-purpose baking mix
½ cup packed brown sugar
⅓ cup granulated sugar
 2 eggs
 2 teaspoons vanilla
½ can evaporated milk
 2 teaspoons margarine or butter,
    melted
 3 large ripe peaches, mashed
¾ teaspoon ground cinnamon

Lightly grease CROCK-POT® Slow Cooker or spray with non-stick cooking spray.

In large bowl, combine baking mix and sugars. Add eggs and vanilla. Stir. Pour in milk and margarine; stir. Mix in peaches and cinnamon until well mixed. Pour into CROCK-POT® Slow Cooker. Cover and cook on Low 6 to 8 hours or on High 3 to 4 hours. Serve warm. Top with vanilla ice cream, if desired.

Makes 4 to 6 servings

SPICED APPLE & CRANBERRY COMPOTE

2½ cups cranberry juice cocktail
 1 package (6 ounces) dried apples
 ½ cup (2 ounces) dried cranberries
 ½ cup Rhine wine or apple juice
 ½ cup honey
 2 cinnamon sticks, broken into
    halves
    Frozen yogurt or ice cream
       (optional)
    Additional cinnamon sticks
       (optional)

Mix juice, apples, cranberries, wine, honey and cinnamon stick halves in slow cooker. Cover and cook on Low 4 to 5 hours or until liquid is absorbed and fruit is tender. Remove and discard cinnamon stick halves. Ladle compote into bowls. Serve warm, at room temperature or chilled with scoop of frozen yogurt or ice cream and garnish with additional cinnamon sticks, if desired.

Makes 6 servings

Spiced Apple & Cranberry Compote

PEACH CRISP

⅔ cup uncooked old-fashioned oats
½ cup granulated sugar
½ cup packed brown sugar
⅓ cup all-purpose baking mix
½ teaspoon ground cinnamon
4 cups sliced peaches

Lightly grease inside of CROCK-POT® Slow Cooker or spray with nonstick cooking spray.

Mix together oats, sugars, baking mix and cinnamon in large bowl. Stir in peaches until well blended. Pour into CROCK-POT® Slow Cooker. Cover and cook on Low 4 to 6 hours.

Makes 4 to 6 servings

Peach Crisp

CHERRY PUDDING

MIXTURE #1

> ¾ cup sugar
> 2 tablespoons plus 1½ teaspoons
> margarine or butter
> 1½ cups all-purpose flour
> ¾ cup evaporated milk
> 1½ teaspoons baking powder
> ¾ teaspoon salt
> ⅛ teaspoon ground cinnamon

MIXTURE #2

> 2 cans (16 ounces each) tart
> cherries and juice
> 2 cups sugar
> ¼ cup all-purpose flour
> ¼ cup margarine or butter, melted
> 1 teaspoon red food color

Lightly grease inside of CROCK-POT® Slow Cooker.

MIXTURE #1

Combine sugar and margarine until crumbly. Add flour, milk, baking powder, salt and cinnamon. Pour into CROCK-POT® Slow Cooker.

MIXTURE #2

Combine all ingredients thoroughly until sugar is dissolved. Pour over Mixture #1 which will rise to the top during baking.

Cover and cook on High 3 to 4 hours or until dough is set and solid. Serve immediately. Top with vanilla ice cream, if desired.

Makes 4 to 6 servings

HONEY ORANGE AND APPLE NUT BREAD PUDDING

2 cups all-purpose flour

²⁄₃ cup plus ¼ cup granulated sugar, divided

3 teaspoons baking powder

1 teaspoon salt

8 tablespoons margarine or butter, cut into cubes

1 cup milk

2 medium tart apples, such as Granny Smith, peeled, cored and cut into cubes

½ cup chopped English walnuts

1½ cups orange juice

½ cup honey

2 tablespoons margarine or butter, melted

1 teaspoon ground cinnamon

1⅓ cups sour cream

4 tablespoons powdered sugar

Lightly grease inside of CROCK-POT® Slow Cooker. In mixing bowl, mix flour, ²⁄₃ cup granulated sugar, baking powder and salt. Cut in margarine with pastry blender or 2 knives until mixture resembles coarse meal. Stir in milk to form stiff dough. Spread dough into bottom of CROCK-POT® Slow Cooker.

Sprinkle apples and walnuts over layer of dough. *Do not stir.*

In another mixing bowl, combine orange juice, honey, remaining ¼ cup granulated sugar, melted margarine and cinnamon. Pour over apple mixture. *Do not stir.*

Cover and cook on High 2 to 3 hours or until apples are tender. *Do not cook on Low.*

In small bowl, whip sour cream and powdered sugar.

Serve warm with dollops of sour cream mixture.

Makes 4 to 6 servings

ENGLISH BREAD PUDDING

16 slices day-old, firm-textured
      white bread (1 small loaf)
1¾ cups milk
  1 package (8 ounces) mixed dried
      fruit, cut into small pieces
  1 medium apple, cored and
      chopped
½ cup chopped nuts
⅓ cup packed brown sugar
¼ cup butter, melted
  1 egg, slightly beaten
  1 teaspoon ground cinnamon
¼ teaspoon ground nutmeg
¼ teaspoon ground cloves

Tear bread, with crusts, into 1- to 2-inch pieces. Place in slow cooker. Pour milk over bread; let soak 30 minutes. Stir in dried fruit, apple and nuts. Combine remaining ingredients in small bowl. Pour over bread mixture. Stir well to blend. Cover and cook on Low 3½ to 4 hours or until skewer inserted in center comes out clean. *Makes 6 to 8 servings*

NOTE: Chopping dried fruits can be difficult. To make the job easier, cut the fruit with kitchen scissors. You can also spray your scissors or chef's knife with nonstick cooking spray before you begin chopping so that the fruit won't stick to the blade.

English Bread Pudding

PINEAPPLE BREAD PUDDING

2 cups sugar
1 cup margarine or butter,
    softened
1 teaspoon ground cinnamon
8 eggs
5 cups toasted bread cubes
2 cans (15¼ ounces each)
    unsweetened crushed
    pineapple, drained
  Chopped pecans (optional)
  Whipped cream (optional)

In bowl, beat sugar, margarine and cinnamon with electric mixer. Add eggs and beat until well blended. Fold bread cubes and pineapple into creamed mixture. Pour into CROCK-POT® Slow Cooker. Cover and cook on Low 6 to 7 hours or on High 3 to 4 hours. Before serving, top with chopped pecans and whipped topping, if desired. Serve warm.

Makes 4 to 6 servings

RICE PUDDING WITH PEARS

4 cups reduced-fat evaporated milk
¾ cup granulated sugar
½ cup short-grain rice, cooked
1 tablespoon cornstarch
2 eggs, beaten
1 can (16 ounces) pears, drained and chopped
1½ teaspoons vanilla extract
1 tablespoon brown sugar
½ teaspoon ground cinnamon

Lightly grease CROCK-POT® Slow Cooker. In mixing bowl, combine evaporated milk, granulated sugar and rice. Stir in cornstarch. Gradually add beaten eggs. Fold in pears and vanilla. Pour into CROCK-POT® Slow Cooker. Combine brown sugar and cinnamon in small bowl. Sprinkle over rice mixture. Cover and cook on High 2 to 3 hours or until pudding is set. Serve.

Makes 8 to 10 servings

STEAMED SOUTHERN SWEET POTATO CUSTARD

1 can (16 ounces) cut sweet
   potatoes, drained
1 can (12 ounces) evaporated
   milk, divided
½ cup packed brown sugar
2 eggs, lightly beaten
1 teaspoon ground cinnamon
½ teaspoon ground ginger
¼ teaspoon salt
   Whipped cream (optional)
   Ground nutmeg (optional)

Process sweet potatoes with about ¼ cup milk in food processor or blender until smooth. Add remaining milk, brown sugar, eggs, cinnamon, ginger and salt; process until well mixed. Pour into *ungreased* 1-quart soufflé dish. Cover tightly with foil. Crumple large sheet (about 15×12 inches) of foil; place in bottom of slow cooker. Pour 2 cups water over foil. Make foil handles (see page 7) and place soufflé dish on top of foil strips.

Transfer dish to slow cooker using foil handles; lay foil strips over top of dish. Cover and cook on High 2½ to 3 hours or until skewer inserted in center comes out clean. Using foil strips, lift dish from slow cooker and transfer to wire rack. Uncover; let stand 30 minutes. Garnish with whipped cream and nutmeg, if desired. *Makes 4 servings*

Steamed Southern Sweet Potato Custard

APPLESAUCE SPICE CAKE

¼ cup butter or margarine
½ cup sugar
 1 egg
½ teaspoon vanilla
¾ cup applesauce
 1 cup all-purpose flour
 1 teaspoon baking soda
¼ teaspoon ground cinnamon
¼ teaspoon ground cloves
¼ teaspoon ground nutmeg
½ cup raisins
½ cup chopped pecans

Cream butter and sugar. Add egg and vanilla; beat well. Beat in applesauce. Combine flour, baking soda and spices; stir into creamed mixture. Blend in raisins and nuts.

Pour into greased and floured Bread 'n Cake Bake Pan and cover. Place in CROCK-POT® Slow Cooker; cover and bake on High 2½ to 4 hours. *Makes 12 servings*

NOTE: Double recipe for 5-quart CROCK-POT® Slow Cooker.

BLACK FOREST CHEESECAKE

¾ cup chocolate graham cracker
  cookies, crushed
3 packages (8 ounces each)
  fat-free cream cheese,
  softened
1½ cups sugar
¾ cup egg substitute
1 cup semisweet chocolate
  morsels, melted
1 container (8 ounces) reduced-
  calorie sour cream
¼ cup unsweetened cocoa powder
1½ teaspoons vanilla
1 can (21 ounces) cherry pie filling
¾ cup reduced-calorie frozen
  whipped topping, thawed

Grease and flour Bread 'n Cake Bake Pan. Spread crushed cookies in bottom of pan; set aside.

Beat cream cheese with electric mixer until fluffy. Gradually add sugar; beat well. Add egg substitute slowly, mixing well. Add melted chocolate, sour cream, cocoa and vanilla until well blended. Pour into prepared Bread 'n Cake Bake Pan. Place lid on pan. Place in CROCK-POT® Slow Cooker. Cover CROCK-POT® Slow Cooker and cook on High 4 hours. Remove from CROCK-POT® Slow Cooker and remove Bread 'n Cake Bake lid. Run knife around edge of pan to release sides. Let cool completely.

Place lid back on Bread 'n Cake Bake Pan and refrigerate cheesecake at least 8 hours. Remove cheesecake from refrigerator, invert pan and run bottom of Bread 'n Cake Bake Pan briefly under warm water. On plate, invert Bread 'n Cake Bake Pan and remove cheesecake. Invert cheesecake right side up onto serving platter. Spread cheesecake with cherry pie filling. Spread with whipped topping or top each slice with dollop of whipped topping. Slice and serve. *Makes 12 servings*

CARROT CAKE

1 cup sugar
²⁄₃ cup vegetable oil
2 eggs
1½ cups all-purpose flour
1 teaspoon baking soda
1 teaspoon ground cinnamon
½ teaspoon salt
1 can (14 ounces) crushed
    pineapple in syrup, drained
¾ cup grated carrots
½ cup chopped nuts
1 teaspoon vanilla

Beat together sugar, oil and eggs. Combine flour, baking soda, cinnamon and salt; add to sugar mixture and beat well. Stir in pineapple, carrots, nuts and vanilla.

Pour into greased and floured Bread 'n Cake Bake Pan. Cover and place in CROCK-POT® Slow Cooker. Cover and bake on High 2½ to 4 hours.   *Makes 12 servings*

CHOCOLATE NUT CAKE

⅔ cup margarine or butter

1½ cups sugar

4 eggs

1 cup prepared instant mashed potatoes

2 cups all-purpose flour

⅔ cup unsweetened cocoa powder

2 teaspoons baking powder

1 teaspoon salt

½ teaspoon ground cinnamon

½ cup milk

½ cup chopped pecans

Grease and flour inside of Bread 'n Cake Bake Pan.

Cream margarine with electric mixer. Beat in sugar and eggs until smooth. Mix in cooled potatoes.

In small bowl, combine flour, cocoa, baking powder, salt and cinnamon. Add to creamed mixture alternately with milk. Fold in pecans. Pour into prepared Bread 'n Cake Bake Pan. Place lid on pan. Set Bread 'n Cake Bake Pan inside CROCK-POT® Slow Cooker. Cover CROCK-POT® Slow Cooker and cook on High 3 to 4 hours or until toothpick inserted comes out clean. Check doneness after 3 hours.

When cake is done remove pan from CROCK-POT® Slow Cooker and let cool 5 to 10 minutes. Invert cake onto plate and invert again onto serving platter. Serve.   *Makes 12 servings*

TRIPLE CHOCOLATE SURPRISE

1 package chocolate cake mix
1 container (8 ounces) sour cream
1 cup chocolate chip morsels
1 cup water
4 eggs
¾ cup vegetable oil
1 package instant chocolate
   pudding mix

Spray CROCK-POT® Slow Cooker with nonstick cooking spray or lightly grease.

Mix cake mix, sour cream, chocolate morsels, water, eggs, oil and pudding mix in bowl by hand. Pour into CROCK-POT® Slow Cooker. Cover and cook on Low 6 to 8 hours or on High 3 to 4 hours. Serve hot or warm with ice cream or whipped cream topping.
Makes 12 servings

Triple Chocolate Surprise

HOT FUDGE CAKE

1 cup plus ¾ cup packed brown
    sugar, divided
1 cup all-purpose flour
¼ cup plus 3 tablespoons
    unsweetened cocoa powder,
    divided
2 teaspoons baking powder
½ teaspoon salt
½ cup milk
2 tablespoons margarine or
    butter, melted
½ teaspoon vanilla
1¾ cups boiling water

Mix 1 cup brown sugar, flour, 3 tablespoons cocoa, baking powder and salt together in mixing bowl. Stir in milk, margarine and vanilla. Spread over bottom of CROCK-POT® Slow Cooker.

In another bowl, mix together remaining ¾ cup brown sugar and remaining ¼ cup cocoa. Sprinkle evenly over mixture in CROCK-POT® Slow Cooker. *Do not stir.*

Pour in boiling water. *Do not stir.* Cover and cook on High 2 to 3 hours until toothpick inserted comes out clean. Serve warm with ice cream or whipped topping, if desired. *Makes 12 servings*

STRAWBERRY CHEESECAKE

CRUST
1¼ cups graham cracker crumbs
¼ cup margarine or butter, melted

CHEESECAKE
2 packages (8 ounces each) plus
    1 (3-ounce) package cream
    cheese, softened
½ cup sugar
2 to 3 tablespoons all-purpose
    flour
3 eggs
½ cup strawberry preserves
1 pint fresh strawberries

Preheat oven to 350°F. Grease and flour inside of Bread 'n Cake Bake Pan.

Mix together graham cracker crumbs and melted margarine. Press into Bread 'n Cake Bake Pan. *Do not cover with lid.* Bake in oven 5 to 7 minutes. Set aside.

With electric mixer, cream softened cream cheese until smooth; mix in sugar and flour. Add eggs, 1 at a time, beating until well blended. Fold in strawberry preserves. Pour over baked crust in Bread 'n Cake Bake Pan. Place lid on pan. Place Bread 'n Cake Bake Pan in CROCK-POT® Slow Cooker and cover. Cook on High 2½ to 3 hours. Remove lid when cheesecake is set. Remove pan from CROCK-POT® Slow Cooker. Allow to cool. Cover and refrigerate 8 hours. Remove and unmold onto plate; invert cheesecake onto serving platter. Top slices with fresh strawberries for serving. *Makes 12 servings*

SOUR CREAM CHOCOLATE CHIP CAKE

½ cup margarine or butter
1 cup sugar
2 eggs
1 cup sour cream
1 teaspoon vanilla
2½ cups all-purpose flour
1 teaspoon baking soda
1 teaspoon baking powder
½ teaspoon salt
1 cup chocolate chips

Grease and flour inside of Bread 'n Cake Bake Pan.

In mixing bowl, cream margarine and sugar with electric mixer. Add eggs and beat well. Mix in sour cream and vanilla.

In small bowl, combine flour, baking soda, baking powder and salt. Add to creamed mixture. Stir in chocolate chips by hand. Pour into prepared Bread 'n Cake Bake Pan. Place lid on pan. Place Bread 'n Cake Bake Pan in CROCK-POT® Slow Cooker. Cover CROCK-POT® Slow Cooker and cook on High 4 hours or until toothpick inserted in center of cake comes out clean.

Makes 12 servings

PEANUT BUTTER AND HOT FUDGE PUDDING CAKE

½ cup all-purpose flour
¾ cup sugar, divided
¾ teaspoon baking powder
⅓ cup milk
 1 tablespoon vegetable oil
½ teaspoon vanilla
¼ cup peanut butter
 3 tablespoons unsweetened cocoa
   powder
 1 cup boiling water

In bowl, combine flour, ¼ cup sugar and baking powder. Add milk, oil and vanilla; stir until smooth. Mix in peanut butter. Pour into CROCK-POT® Slow Cooker.

In same mixing bowl, stir together remaining ½ cup sugar and cocoa powder. Gradually stir in boiling water. Pour mixture over batter in CROCK-POT® Slow Cooker. *Do not stir.*

Cover and cook on High 2 to 3 hours or until toothpick inserted comes out clean. Serve warm with vanilla ice cream, hot fudge sauce and nuts. *Makes 4 to 6 servings*

Slow Cooker

INDEX

INDEX

INDEX

INDEX

INDEX

INDEX

METRIC CONVERSION CHART

VOLUME MEASUREMENTS (dry)

$1/8$ teaspoon = 0.5 mL
$1/4$ teaspoon = 1 mL
$1/2$ teaspoon = 2 mL
$3/4$ teaspoon = 4 mL
1 teaspoon = 5 mL
1 tablespoon = 15 mL
2 tablespoons = 30 mL
$1/4$ cup = 60 mL
$1/3$ cup = 75 mL
$1/2$ cup = 125 mL
$2/3$ cup = 150 mL
$3/4$ cup = 175 mL
1 cup = 250 mL
2 cups = 1 pint = 500 mL
3 cups = 750 mL
4 cups = 1 quart = 1 L

VOLUME MEASUREMENTS (fluid)

1 fluid ounce (2 tablespoons) = 30 mL
4 fluid ounces ($1/2$ cup) = 125 mL
8 fluid ounces (1 cup) = 250 mL
12 fluid ounces ($1 1/2$ cups) = 375 mL
16 fluid ounces (2 cups) = 500 mL

WEIGHTS (mass)

$1/2$ ounce = 15 g
1 ounce = 30 g
3 ounces = 90 g
4 ounces = 120 g
8 ounces = 225 g
10 ounces = 285 g
12 ounces = 360 g
16 ounces = 1 pound = 450 g

DIMENSIONS

$1/16$ inch = 2 mm
$1/8$ inch = 3 mm
$1/4$ inch = 6 mm
$1/2$ inch = 1.5 cm
$3/4$ inch = 2 cm
1 inch = 2.5 cm

OVEN TEMPERATURES

250°F = 120°C
275°F = 140°C
300°F = 150°C
325°F = 160°C
350°F = 180°C
375°F = 190°C
400°F = 200°C
425°F = 220°C
450°F = 230°C

BAKING PAN SIZES

Utensil	Size in Inches/Quarts	Metric Volume	Size in Centimeters
Baking or Cake Pan (square or rectangular)	8×8×2	2 L	20×20×5
	9×9×2	2.5 L	23×23×5
	12×8×2	3 L	30×20×5
	13×9×2	3.5 L	33×23×5
Loaf Pan	8×4×3	1.5 L	20×10×7
	9×5×3	2 L	23×13×7
Round Layer Cake Pan	8×1½	1.2 L	20×4
	9×1½	1.5 L	23×4
Pie Plate	8×1¼	750 mL	20×3
	9×1¼	1 L	23×3
Baking Dish or Casserole	1 quart	1 L	—
	1½ quart	1.5 L	—
	2 quart	2 L	—